Jacksonville

UNITED STATES DEPARTMENT OF THE INTERIOR
WASHINGTON, D. C.

Jacksonville Historic District

Oregon

is hereby designated a

REGISTERED NATIONAL HISTORIC LANDMARK

*Under the Provisions of the
Historic Sites Act of August 21, 1935.
This Site Possesses Exceptional Value in
Commemorating and Illustrating the
History of the United States of America.*

Secretary of the Interior

Director, National Park Service

Jacksonville
Oregon

Antique Town in a Modern Age

Documentary

Bert and Margie Webber

WEBB RESEARCH GROUP
Books About the Oregon Country

Some of the material in this book appeared in
Jacksonville, Oregon,
The Making of a National Historic Landmark
Copyright © Bert Webber 1978
(Out-of-Print)

Cover Photograph by Bert Webber:
Bill and Karen Shulmans'
"Jacksonville Carriage Service" at its
terminal at the Orth Building on S. Oregon Street

Published by:
WEBB RESEARCH GROUP
Books About the Oregon Country
P. O. Box 314 Medford, Oregon 97501

Library of Congress Cataloging in Publications Data:

Webber, Bert
Jacksonville, Oregon : antique town in a modern age :
documentary / Bert and Margie Webber.
p.   cm.
Includes bibliographical references and index.
ISBN 0-936738-41-3
1. Jacksonville (Or.)–History. I. Webber, Margie. II. Title.
F884.J32W4197   1993   93-3526
979.5'27–dc20   CIP

Contents

Picture overleaf: Jacksonville, Oregon photographed in 1990 by Bert Webber

Labels on image: Medford→, Museum, California St., Cemetery, Post office, U.S. Hotel, Orth Bldg.

Jacksonville, Oregon
(Camera faces to the northwest)

Introduction and Acknowledgments

Jacksonville intrigued us from the very start. Our first visit was by accident, it was about 3 in the morning, and we were lost! The rented house we were looking for was about two miles back on a side road. We'd missed the turn. It was some days later before we realized where we'd been after we described the little town, with all the old buildings, to an acquaintance. Although it has not been our fortune to live there, the town is only minutes away from our home so visits are not unduly restricted. It's our favorite place to escort visitors.

What we did not learn about the town and its people from casual visits, we have surely learned during the research for the present book.

This book is intended as a popular volume for general reading but at the same time, we have tried for historical accuracy. It is true here as with our other books, the background gleaned is immense when weighed against what finally emerges in print.

We talked informally with dozens of folks, and had formal interview appointments with others. We were in and out of the Reference Department of the Jackson County Library System in Medford on a continuing basis. The librarians knew where data was kept on subjects we asked about and produced it with friendly professionalism whether we were there in person or at the end of a telephone line.

In the Jacksonville library we were shown artifacts that came with the building well over 100 years ago. We offer our heartfelt thanks to all of these librarians.

We quickly found the "center of contemporary information" in Jacksonville to be the City Hall, where Doris Crofoot fielded our questions with interest and precision, sometimes pointing out of a window and down the street toward what we were after. Now that's very real help for which we are thankful.

Don Wendt receives a thank you and a handshake for his

assistance with recollections of life in the town where he grew up and still calls home. As publisher of the Jacksonville *Nugget* (and an often city councilman) Don willingly provided much background and covered some matters about which we did not know to ask.

Jacksonville's "Hungry '30's" backyard mining history is most colorful and was put together as we have it, after much help from fellows who were there: The late Wes Hartman was one. We walked and drove the town and surrounding area stopping to view, then draw in locations of old mine shafts and tunnels under streets as he recalled them. Wes had been City Mining Inspector and Mayor. With Bill Dobbyn we went to Jackson Creek to look at the site where his dredge pulled out well over $1,000 of gold in some weeks.

A very special acknowledgement and thanks to Mrs. A. C. Van Galder, who talked with us then showed us "dips" in her lawn that were sites of former mine shafts.

Also of assistance on the mining chapter was Novus Webb, who studied the mining history then put together the illustrated "Backyard Mining in Jacksonville" map published by the Southern Oregon Historical Society. Thank you all.

The treks we made through the brush and tall grass seeking evidence of the Rogue River Valley Railroad, and the people we talked with about that operation made the subject most exciting. We found little had been written and of that, it was sometimes faulty. But recollections were sharp from the late M. Dale Newton, railway historian and map maker who backed his comments with maps, photographs, and artifacts some of which are heretofore unpublished. And Newton was the one who pointed out the locations of many old rails used as street sign posts in Medford.

Wes Hartman rode that train many times – testified and helped us conclude that the right-of-way was no where near the "steep grade" others wrote about it traversing. Alvin Bowman, once Mayor and later land developer, validated our search for the place where the rails crossed Daisy Creek then proceeded east near Beverly Way. Stan Hobbs of the State Highway Engineer's Office, Medford, produced an old map which, early in our study, turned our heads in the direction that, really, there was no "steep grade" on the railroad between Medford and Jacksonville afterall. Fellows, thanks to you we have the record and story as straight as we think it can be made.

There are so many persons who helped in various ways as several managers, over time, of Pacific Northwest Bell Telephone, and later U.S. West, who sought data from a rare 1899 telephone book for us which added the little extra touch of flavor.

There was Rev. E. Melvin Kessinger and the Session of the First Presbyterian Church that permitted the two of us to scramble up narrow ladders into the belfry to photograph that great bell which has been announcing services almost continuously, weekly, for over 100 years. His successor, Dr. Lawrence Jung has continued the assistance whenever we called on him.

There have been a number of Parish priests and sextons associated with St. Joseph's Church who allowed us access into Parish archives and answered our questions. We appreciate the time they took which helped us with this book. Thank you.

When one wants to locate a marker in a cemetery in a small town, it's important to meet the sexton, Wayne Maxon, to whom we are indebted for locating monuments pertinent to our story that we'd otherwise would have had to search for days.

Our research for facts and opinions for this book has extended over more than twenty years. Many of the folks we talked with, old-timers, have passed on. We remember them now.

We believe that historic postmarks add so much to the spirit of historical studies so we asked postal historian Leonard Lukens to loan some of his choice "Jacksonville" cancellations which he graciously did.

We thank Dennice Bateman, bibliophile and knowledgeable Manager of the Jacksonville Information Center's office in the historic Jacksonville railroad depot, who graciously reviewed the manuscript.

The authors welcome constructive comments which can be sent in care of the publisher whose address is shown on page iv.

Bert and Margie Webber
Central Point, Oregon

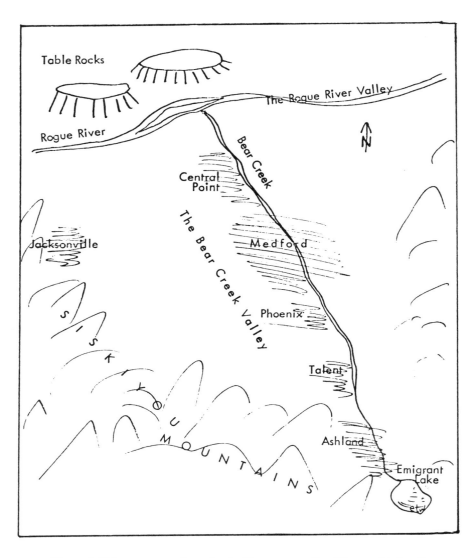

Though it is common to refer to the area as the "Rogue Valley," to be more precise Jacksonville is in the "Bear Creek valley."

1.
In The Beginning

Oregon's historic landmark district in Jacksonville boasts a main street whose store buildings are over 100 years old and face on a street which is very probably lined with gold.

The city, about five miles west of Medford and in the foothills of the Siskiyou Mountains, got its start when gold was discovered in the area in 1851. Jacksonville is the oldest town in Southern Oregon and is a fascinating place to visit.

By the early 1850's, gold was the biggest news throughout the mountainous west. The strike had been immense near Sacramento and miners, who seldom stayed in one place very long, wandered north prospecting streams as they traveled. James Cluggage and John R. Pool found gold in Daisy Creek (now within the city of Jacksonville) in Oregon, in the foothills of the Siskiyou Mountains. As the word got out, miners flocked to the area and a shanty town, Table Rock City – later Jacksonville – came into being.

The site of Jacksonville was in an almost unpopulated area. Oregon's first community was Astoria, at the mouth of the Columbia River on its south bank, then settlements, along the river sprang up near the confluence with the Willamette River. These were Vancouver, in what later became Washington State, and on the Oregon side the major towns of Portland, Milwaukie, and Oregon City.*

The Willamette Valley was known for its fertile soil thus many immigrants, who sought new homes and wanted to farm, headed there in the great overland crossings. The boisterous shanty town of Jacksonville was almost 300 miles away on the

*For an excellent account of the start of Oregon City, the early settlement that marked the western end of the Oregon Trail as well as details about Oregon City today, see, *Oregon City (By Way of the Barlow Road) At the End of the National Historic Oregon Trail.* See bibliography.

Earliest known picture of Jacksonville, probably late 1853, as the Methodist Church is without its steeple (white building in center). Shanty buildings in foreground were in "Chinatown."

raw frontier of Oregon and had only transient white population until the discovery of gold.

A. G. Walling, writing in his *History of Southern Oregon* (published in 1884) recorded:

> Nowhere else in America, possibly not in the world, have the forces of nature so conspired to beautify and render a region thoroughly delightful as [here].

Both Daisy Creek and Jackson Creek flow through the town. A few miles east is Bear Creek, the major drainage of the area which empties into the Rogue River about eight miles to the north. Though it is common to refer to the area as the "Rogue Valley," to be more precise this is the Bear Creek Valley.

In early days, access to Jacksonville was rough for there are mountains on all sides. Those on the south rise to over 7,000 feet elevation with the passes through them over 4,000 feet high. Weather is mild with storm clouds spilling most of the rain on the

Jacksonville in mid-18590's. Note steeple on church, the church faces west on 4th Street. White "pyramid" near church is tent built of split lumber by Rev. Joseph S. Smith, first Methodist minister and predates church. "Tent" was used as community hall, for "court," as well as sermons. Long white building is Robinson House, a hotel with extension (compare with earlier town photograph (page 12). White building on far right is Jackson County's first Court House.

western slopes, then the clouds float over the valley to shower again on the next range.

Despite the fact that Jackson County was soon astride the stage coach route between Sacramento and the Willamette Valley, as well as being on the route of the South Road (Applegate Trail) from the mid-west, the area was considered far too remote a region for much early development. Of course a major influx followed the electrifying news of "Gold"!* Some early farmers had settled here and found ready markets for their produce among the miners of Jacksonville. From a village of random tents, the first log cabin appeared in 1852 and businesses started. A large tent served as a general store where the most common goods to trade for gold dust were whiskey, tools and heavy clothing.

The mines were described as "rich." Gambling, rough talk and booze were common while the sight of a woman – there were only five in the village – was a curiosity. Merchants from afar got

---

* See bibliography for the book *Gold Mining in Oregon Past and Present*.

Southeast section of Jacksonville about 1880. I.O.O.F. hall marked "A."

the scent of potential business among the miners – showed up. It was not long before several hundred people referred to Jacksonville as "home" during the week, but this swelled by several hundreds more on weekends as miners streamed into town from the hills. They headed for saloons and card rooms (some of which had "back-room" attractions – women – and the horse races. Business was brisk in the tent stores.

One enterprising fellow, John Ross, had roamed the frontier for years until he learned of the gold strike at Jacksonville. He bought a herd of cattle in the Willamette Valley, moved them to ground near Jacksonville, then he sold them to the miners as food.

In general, there appears to have been three types of people in early Jacksonville. 1) miners, 2) saloon and store keepers, 3) farmers. More often than not, farmers dealt directly with miners selling not only garden produce but beef, butter, eggs and pork. A blacksmith became a necessity and several smithies set up their shops. The first plow manufactured in the Rogue Valley came from one of these forges.

While miners roared in and out of town, others came to settle, do business and start families. Among them was 33-year-old Peter Britt to be followed shortly by Cornelius C. Beekman, about 25.

More than a few "well-disposed persons" had become prospectors and when they rested on weekends, their homes became

14

Monument at corner S. Oregon and Applegate Streets commemorates discovery of gold here in 1851.

stopping places for itinerant preachers. Among these better-educated was Benjamin Franklin Dowell who had been schooled at the University of Virginia as a lawyer. But in Jacksonville he ran a pack train.

There was no organized law enforcement therefore people were forced to cooperate for their mutual protection. This was specifically because the Indians, whose way of life had been interrupted by whitemen, were very unsettled.

15

Early post card showing "Hydraulic Mining in Jackson County, Oregon." Date unknown but postmarked at Tablerock, Oregon, 1906.

The Honorable Matthew P. Deady, United States District Judge for Oregon Territory by Presidential Appointment, held his first court in Jacksonville on September 5, 1853. One of the officers of his court was Lafayette F. Grover. He was a Lieutenant in the 1853 Rogue Indian War and went on to become the first U. S. Representative from the new State of Oregon, a Governor of Oregon, then U.S. Senator from Oregon.

Early in 1853, settlers included some who wished to start a Methodist Church. Among the very active in this movement was Rev. Joseph S. Smith (later a Representative to Congress), who had been assigned to the new village of Jacksonville, He arrived with his wife, and two other ladies, Miss Overbeck and Miss Emma Royal. These two women took to the mining camps and saloons to solicit money for building a church. In town, money was also collected from the "sporting fraternity" who in their own words were "hedging against bad fortune in the world to come."

In 1854, the Methodists built their church facing west on 4th Street. It was the first church in town. Later they turned it to face on 5th Street where the building, but not the Methodists, remains to the present time.

In the business world of the village, express service was opened to San Francisco via Yreka. Cornelius Beekman (called "Beek" by his friends) rode horseback carrying pouches of gold dust from the miners and later carried letters. Interestingly, he traveled alone, was never held up, and crossed the Siskiyou mountains at night. He was later appointed Wells Fargo Agent for Jacksonville and eventually, in 1857, founded the first bank in Southern Oregon. *

Beekman became one of Jacksonville's most distinguished and philanthropic citizens.

The first child was born in Jacksonville on August 5, 1853 to Doctor and Mrs. McCully. It was noted by one historian that the boy, who was named James Cluggage McCully for the town's founder, became the special pride of many miners and traders – all claiming to be godfathers –

...and made it their especial business to spoil the graceless little scamp and teach him lessons that required years of Sunday School attendance to eradicate.

It should be pointed out that the major type of mining in Jacksonville at this time was "placer" mining. Such mining can be done when gold-bearing sand and gravel settle out from rapidly moving streams. Panning for gold requires a wide, flat pan into which a few handfuls of silt from the bottom of the creek, or dry earth from a suitable hillside (which the prospector hopes contains gold), and an amount of water have been placed. By swirling the contents, the miner washes the dirt, gravel and sand over the edge of the pan leaving any heavy matter, including gold, in the pan. After several washings of the same handful of earth, only gold and other heavy metals are left. "Nuggets," as different from "dust," can be easily picked out of the pan with fingers. If there is only dust present, continuous washing is needed to force all of the final sands over the edge of the pan. When only the gold dust remains, the miner carefully removes the particles, sometimes

---

*Beekman's bank (1857) predates the Ladd & Tilton Bank in Oregon City (1859) therefore is Oregon's first bank. But so-called experts about Oregon's banking industry, namely officials of U. S. National Bank of Oregon, discount Beekman's enterprise as he was not "incorporated" and operated his bank differently than the "experts" deemed proper. Ladd & Tilton eventually became U. S. National Bank of Oregon. See Chapter 9. See bibliography.

with tweezers, or a knife blade, from the pan.*

Traditionally, gold prospectors work a stream looking for "color" only for a short time in any one spot. They move about dipping their pans here and there. If a stream produces, they stay until they can't find any more. In the California strike, placer mining lasted just a short while until surface gold in the streams was panned out. In Jacksonville, the same procedure was followed with many miners moving on after a relatively short stay. As miners left, others came in. The turnover does not seem to be recorded but it was heavy. White miners, when compared with Chinese miners, did an incomplete job. Whites seemed to discourage easily then moved on but the Chinese, as we shall see, reworked several times over the very spots which whites had abandoned.

Summer of 1853 was most eventful. Additional gold discoveries brought more and more people. It was a season of great prosperity. Goods for sale to the miners were mule-train packed over 100 miles from the seaport at Crescent City, California.

An uneasy treaty was made with the Indians to patch up past quarrels thus many felt that Indian trouble was lessened.**

Much gold as well as boisterous miners poured into Jacksonville and summer nights were never quiet. Walling wrote:

There never was a mining camp where personal liberty was less restrained, better enjoyed or less abused than in Jacksonville in '53.

With "civilization" growing in this shanty town in the foothills of the Siskiyou mountains, crime was also growing. Rape, theft, murder, filled the docket of the court. Indian trouble was brewing following the arrest of three Indians, each on separate murder charges. Each Indian was tried and found guilty then all three were publicly hanged. Jacksonville was surely no quiet, country village at this time although as we noted from Walling, he didn't see it quite that way.

Life was hard work day after day in this far-flung corner of

---

* Readers interested in details of the history of gold mining in Oregon and specifically how to pan for gold, are referred to *Gold Mining In Oregon – Past and Present.* See bibliography.

** Authors' note: The present book will mention the Rogue Indian wars only in passing. See: Appendix A for an opinion at the time.

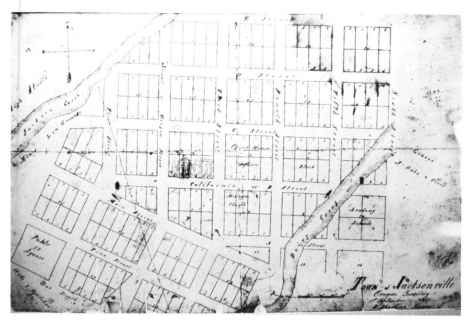

Earliest plat of Jacksonville filed with County Commissioners 1 September 1852.

America and the settlers, as well as the miners, longed for their friends and loved ones who had remained at home thousands of miles away. Their contact with the "doings" of the world they had left behind was eagerly kept via mail-order newspapers.

Welborn Beeson confided to his diary on Dec. 15, 1853, that he had struck a deal with a neighbor, John Meall, for each to fetch the others' papers and letters from Jacksonville when either was in that village. Beeson lived on his father's farm near what is now the City of Talent, about ten miles southeast. At one point, Beeson wrote he hated to spend the dollar for a subscription to a distant paper as money was very dear, but he felt he couldn't get along without it.

After the passage of the Donation Land Act which promised free, fertile farm land most of which was covered by heavy trees, the population increased with those who wanted to build homes and stay.

As gold mining declined, skeptics announced the end of the town was near. True, the restless left but that was nothing new. Some still puttered around the creeks seeking gold but many took

19

Chinatown in the 1850's along this block on Main Street. At this writing, area is in lawn, shrubs and trees.

Gin Lin, a wealthy Chinese miner who employed many dozens of his countrymen in his operations in the hills above Jacksonville.

jobs with businesses which were starting to grow. The business-men of the town began to look to the farmers for support.

The adjustment from a local "gold dust standard" to an econo-my supported by less immediately-available cash, but from steadily-employed farmers, was uneasy. The mines had been the initial incentive for many of the agricultural ventures and when the farmers did their buying, it was with gold dust or coin realized from direct sales to the miners. Few farmers had ready cash. It took a farmer many weeks, sometimes months of dawn-to-dark toil from seeding to the harvesting of his crop. For orchards, the investment was even greater with no proceeds for several years.

But farmers were prospering more than most realized. After the first few hard winters, the valley became largely self-suf-ficient. By the time the mines ran out – about ten years – farmers were looking for out-of-area markets. Centers-of-interest were appearing in the county. Ashland Mills and Phoenix had flour mills. Jacksonville became the banking and shipping center, was the county seat and had a newspaper, the *Table Rock Sentinel*. As we shall see, it was not long before a brick kiln was set up west of town. (Medford had not yet been founded and was still some years in the distance.) There were nearly a dozen merchants with substantial establishments. There were many saloons and even a bowling alley!

21

An hotel, the Robinson House – on the site of the present United States Hotel – catered to all who were stuck in town overnight. In addition, there was a boarding house of a more elite nature (in which some of the courtesans abided). There were many small businesses including two bakeries, a stable and a furniture maker.

In contrast to the mule packers and miners, people in town took on a refinement in manners of dress. "Boiled shirts" became the fashion for young gents if they were to make any headway with an increasing crop of young ladies.

Emma Royal, who had been one of the money collectors for funds to build the Methodist Church, opened the first school in the winter of 1853 and funded it in part by returning to the miners for more gold dust contributions.

Winters were severe. With narrow trails and no roads, snow obscured the landscape and supplies usually ran low. Salt and flour were always short in winter so neighbors shared for as long as supplies lasted.

PRICES IN JACKSONVILLE MAY 27, 1854			
Men's Shoes $2.50	Shirts $1	Pants $2	Muslin 25¢ yd
Milk Pail $1	Sharpening stone $1	Sack of salt $1	
Sugar 34¢ lb.	Calico 24¢ yd	Nails 35¢ lb.	

On September 9, 1854, Welborn Beeson hauled farm produce to Jacksonville to sell. He got 12½¢ lb. for 600 lbs. of flour. He was paid 6¢ lb. for 300 lbs. potatoes.

Suitable clay had been found west of Jacksonville and a brick kiln was set up, resulting in the first brick building being constructed in 1854. (That building stood twenty years then burned and the brick walls collapsed.)

The Methodist Church and Miss Emma Royal's school prospered, although that first school term lasted only one month. As Walling wrote concerning the first Roman Catholic overtures in the area:

It would have been strange, indeed, if so promising a field had been overlooked by the Roman Catholic archbishop of Oregon.

Rev. Fr. James Croke, a missionary of Oregon's archdiocese, arrived in Jacksonville in September 1853 for a look-see. While in

22

The first school was held here. The building has been remodeled a number of times.

the village he celebrated mass in a private residence. Here, historian Walling claims Fr. Croke found "a strong steadfast and faithful Catholic society." But Father Croke's personal report to his headquarters described the Jacksonville "parish" in slightly stronger words:

> The Catholics here are so few and in general so lukewarm that it requires some time for a priest to hunt them out [there being] only 100 Catholic adults and 5 minors.

The second brick building in Jacksonville came into existence also in 1854 when the Brunner Brothers erected it for their store. This building still stands and houses, on a lease at this writing, the Jacksonville Branch of the Jackson County Library System. An original writing desk remains in the building and is used daily by librarian and patrons.

Another brick building, the Masonic Lodge, was built in 1855.*

A long feared and bloody war between the Indians and the settlers became a reality when unsettled Indians and troublesome whites met in deadly skirmishes throughout the valley and into the

---

* The history of the Masonic Lodge in Jacksonville is preserved in the book *The Lodge, Jacksonville Masonic Fraternities (Oregon)*. See bibliography.

23

Brunner Building is oldest brick building in town and presently houses the Jacksonville Branch of the Jackson County Library System. Orth Building (lower right) in 1982. For present view see front cover.

Artists love to picture spirited horses racing ahead of a loaded stage coach. In reality, coach could seat only 9 passengers, usually none on top other than driver and "shotgun" in bench seat.

foothills of the Siskiyous. There was no militia to call so the men left wives and firesides to shoulder what arms they could muster to fight Indians. On October 8, a company, organized at Jacksonville, attacked an Indian camp on Butte Creek and killed most of the band, which consisted mostly of old men, women and children. This caused the Indians to go on the warpath then they killed at least 23 whites immediately thereafter.

There never was an attack in Jacksonville itself, but the anxiety, especially among the wives and young girls who imagined themselves being carried off by what they believed would be uncouth, sweat-stained savages, was continual. When there were threats of Indian attacks, Jacksonville folklore tells that the women often barricaded themselves in Brunner's brick store. The wives wanted their men to stay home and they said so.

Some of these women met in an indignation meeting in the Methodist Church about their men abandoning them and roaring around fields looking for Indians. The women passed a resolution denouncing their men's actions. Showing little respect for their ladies' wrath, some fellows late one night hoisted a petticoat to the town's flag pole. It was later hauled down amidst a flurry of the women.

Welborn Beeson's Diary:
April 27, 1855
    We Went to Jacksonville. Took potatoes butter and eggs. We heard a speech at the Robison *(sic)* [Dr. Robertson] house by Gen. Joseph Lane, who is a candidate for Representative to Congress. He is a "red man" with whiskey roses all on his nose. He is a Demicrat *(sic)*. We also heard a speech from Gen. Gainer, a Whig Candidate fir the same he is a white haired old man living on the Columbia [River]. It rained on us as we came home.

Within four years, Jacksonville had four lawyers, several doctors and a number of merchants of a general variety. Leaders were beginning to emerge who would become the mainstay of the community both in business and politics.

Early religious leaders centered on Jacksonville due to its larger population, but soon worked throughout the county. The Methodists, Catholics, Presbyterians and Baptists came, all wanting to build permanent establishments.*

The Baptists however, never gained a foothold in town and there is no Baptist Church in Jacksonville at this writing. The Baptists did, however, build a small church in May 1853 under the direction of missionary James Read, several miles northeast of town in the vicinity of the promontories, Table Rocks. The flock numbered just 19.

Myron Stearns followed the Rev. Mr. Read the next year and set up a circuit that went as far as the foothills of the Siskiyous. His work paid off for in two years his congregation reached 24 but not all of it ever met in the same place at the same time. For its own unique reasons, in 1856 the American Baptist Home Missionary Society in the east withdrew its support. Pastor Stearns was forced to take up farming in order to eat. As Farnham put it:

> This collapse of missionary aid [money] launched Jackson County Baptists upon a generation of impotence. Stearns was unable to replace those restless persons who left each year and his Sunday Schools collapsed.

We will discuss other religious interests shortly.

Jacksonville, despite its growth and genesis of stability, was still a frontier town. Railroads were becoming numerous in the

---

* There were many instances of bickerings between the Methodists and Catholics in the form of public orations by the clergy of each group. The newspapers picked up on these sometimes taking sides, sometimes being neutral. For an illuminating discussion, see Farnam in bibliography.

26

Visiting girls stop to admire Bill Shulman's team of horses at the Jacksonville Carriage Service stop at the Orth Building.

east, but to get in or out of "J'ville," one could walk, ride a horse – possibly with a wagon – or take a stage coach. Riding the stage, with its attendant uncomfortable mountain passes, strained the stoutest horses and the stress limits of passengers. Summers were unbearable with dust, and winters were freezing to all who sat and bounced or became "seasick" with the sway. None but the hardiest or those whose business absolutely required it, took the stage. □

THE TABLE ROCK SENTINEL.

BY TVAULT & BLAKELY.]

INDEPENDENT ON ALL SUBJECTS; DEVOTED TO THE BEST INTEREST OF SOUTHERN OREGON.

[TERMS—$5 00 PER ANNUM.

Volume 1.

JACKSONVILLE, OREGON, SATURDAY, MAY 24, 1856.

Number 27.

THE TABLE ROCK SENTINEL

IS PUBLISHED EVERY SATURDAY, BY

TVAULT & BLAKELY.

Terms—In Advance:
One copy, for one year, $5 00.
"   "   six months, $3 00.
"   "   three months, $2 00.

WE herewith present to the following rates: One square of twelve lines or less, three insertions, $3 00; each subsequent insertion, $1 00. A liberal deduction made to yearly advertisers.

ADVERTISEMENTS inserted at the following rates: One square of twelve lines or less, for one year, $30; to persons who advertise to the extent of three squares or more, a reduction of 20 per cent. will be made.

☞ The number of insertions must be distinctly marked on the margin, otherwise they will be continued till forbidden, and charged accordingly.

China News.

Our exchanges by the Live Yankee did not come to hand till yesterday morning.—We cannot find any news of importance in them, except the following from the Hong Kong Register of the 11th March:

The American Minister's Bowman.—We have been informed that some amusing epistolary diplomatic by-play has lately taken place between H. E. Dr. Parker, the American Commissioner, and Hip, the Viceroy of Canton. We have not seen the correspondence, but it has been made public enough in Canton, where it has been freely commented upon. The cases, as we have heard it, is as follows:

On the Commissioner's arrival by the December mail, H. E. addressed a communication to Hip, informing him of the having entered upon the duties of his office as Commissioner from the United States—expressing his pleasure at finding the country free from the civil dissensions which had existed at the departure—assuring Hip of the high...

News Items Crowded Out Last Week.

Distressing Accident.— A very distressing accident occurred yesterday afternoon, at half-past five o'clock, at Pacific Garden, which cast a shadow over the Turner's Festival. A man named Charles Degers and a Hollander, name unknown, were engaged in firing a salute with a brass four-pounder on the grass plat in front of the garden. They had fired two rounds and were ramming home the cartridge for the third discharge when the charge exploded, horribly mutilating both the parties. Degers had his right hand blown entirely off, lost his left arm below the elbow joint, besides the muscle of his left shoulder, the fleshy portion of his throat, and a wound in the left breast. The Hollander had both of his hands blown off, but was not injured otherwise bodily. The wounded men presented a most pitiful spectacle. The Chief Engineer, Mr. Nuttman, and the Assistants, Mr. Devoe, Mr. Walsh, the Foreman of Engine Company No. 8, together with the reporters of the press and other active gentlemen present, rendered prompt and sympathetic attention to the wounded men. Degers was carried to the German Benevolent Infirmary, on Mission street, near Third, and received the best medical attention by Dr. Sawyer, Physician to the Fire Department, assisted by Drs. C. J. Bryant and J. J. Cushing. At a late hour last evening he was still alive, although his recovery under such mutilation is almost impossible. The Hollander was taken to a private house, where he is under the treatment of Drs. Gray and Rabe. It is more than probable he will recover.—S.F. Herald, 6th.

"Some Shaking."

Tom is a queer genius, and lots of some fall come occasionally. He visited us the other day in our custom, with a

"How do you do, old fellow?"

"Hallo, Tom," said we, "where have you been so long?"

"Why, sir, I have been down on Sevier River, in Ann Arundel county, taking shanghai notes on the riffle and rivers."

"Ah, indeed; are they very bad down there?"

"Rather bad," said Tom, dryly. "There is one place where they have been attempting to build a brick house for eight weeks—well, the other day, as the hands were putting up the bricks preparatory to finishing it, they were taken with a chill and shook the house completely down, and kept on shaking till the bricks were dust of the finest quality! Just at that juncture the chills came on with renewed force and, they commenced shaking up the dust with such gusto that they were entirely consumed in it, and the people of the neighborhood thought the sun was in an eclipse."

"Can't believe anything like that, Tom."

"It's a fact," said Tom, and resumed:

"There's a farmer down there, who, in apple-picking season, took his niggers out to the orchard and sets one of them under a tree on the ground."

"Incredible!" said we, holding our sides with both hands.

"Fact," said Tom, "they keep a man alongside of each negro to take him away as soon as the fruit is off, for fear he will shake the tree down."

Tom continued, "Mr. S——, friend of mine, had a carpenter, who was engaged a few days ago in covering the roof of a house with shingles. Just as he was finishing the chill came on and he shook every shingle off the roof. Some of them are repeat...

Glad I didn't get Married.— We take the following from the Evening Bulletin of the 10th inst.:

"Well, I'm an old maid! Not the only one, either, thank Heaven! To be sure, there's not superabundance in San Francisco—reasons enough why there ain't, too. I do really believe it's the greatest market for girls, young or old, in the known world. Now there isn't a city, town or village this side the Himalayas, but what has shipped more or less of this stock—always ready sale—plenty of Degers, with the cash in hand. 'Wasn't I' mad, 'after having my stomach turned inside out, on that rolling, shaking George Law—almost breaking my neck up and down those fearful mountains, on a cross-grained, supernatural mule, and then drawing the breath of life three whole weeks in a little square place, half as large as a little square place,—half as large as an elephant's pen, say,—wasn't I mad when I got here, to find there wasn't a young man, widower or bachelor in the whole place worth having! Now, I'm as reasonable a woman as ever was born, since Mrs. Eve let the light of her eye shine upon poor lonely Adam, but I'll no more think of marrying that molten calf the Good Book tells about! No! I! I've got a few hundred left yet—if it did cost a heap to rig out, and land here! I am glad enough I wasn't in a hurry. The best thing I ever did in all my life, was in taking care of some of my friends! An old maid, eh?—yes, indeed! Do you think I'd sell my freedom to a regular California! I've always had some domestic notions, whenever matrimony was thought of. What marry a man...

A Hard Shell Baptist Sermon.—The Baltimore American has received from a friend in Lexington, Ky., the following "Hard Shell Sermon," which he avows to be genuine. It almost equals, in absence of argument, and strict adherence to the text, the "spontaneous efforts" of the clerical force who played upon a "harp of a thousand strings:"

"My brethring: The Scriptures tell us, we are burred with Christ by baptism.— 'Burred,' my friends, not 'sprinkled' by baptism.

"Suppose that one of you had lost your little darter, and you had laid her out, and prepared her for the grave; and your neighbor had come in and said: 'Friend, we will take thy child and bury it,' and afterward, when you went out to see the grave of your little one, you found they had laid her down and sprinkled a little earth over her! What would you have think of them?

"Suppose, again, that in the fall of the year, you had dug your potatoes, your turnips, your parsnips and your other roots for winter's use, and had dug a trench to bury 'em in; and you had said to your servant: 'Sally, take the turnips, parsnips and other roots; and afterward, when you walked forth to see that all were secure for the winter's use, you had found them that they had just sprinkled a little dirt on them! What my friends would you have done? I rather suppose, my dear brethren, you would ha' trod the virtues of the sarvint!

"But they are not a bit worse than those poor, ignorant, benighted Episcopalians and Presbyterian and Methodists, who sprinkle a little water on one another and call it baptism.'"

FUN, FLIRT AND NONSENSE.
(Principally Scissors.)

☞ What do we often drop, but never stoop to pick up? A hint.

Men are called sons of guns because they all go off—some time or other.

☞ The bumps raised on a man's head by a cudgel are called frag-nological developments.

☞ What marine occurrence is a man like who lives idly upon his friends? A sponge.

A correspondent asks whether the "ridge of the nose" is a aqueous or wooden bridge.

If you wish to know whether anybody is superior to the projections of the world, ask him to draw a breath for you.

☞ A lazy fellow down South spells Tennessee thus: 10ac. He is the same fellow who spells Andrew Jackson thus—Anjm.

☞ A recent philosopher discovers a method to avoid being damned. "How! how?" we hear everybody asking. Never run in debt.

Says the lovely Ellen to the bewitching Fanny, "why is a new baby like a corn tail? Fanny blushed as she answered, "because it was never seen before."

"Mr. Smith, you said you boarded at the Columbian Hotel six months, did you foot your bill?" "No, sir; but it amounted to your board." No, sir; but it amounted to some thing—the landlord fooled me."

An Irishman, writing to a friend from the West, remarked, that "Pork is so plenty here that every third man you meet is a hog."

A correspondent asks, whether the great lady who fell in love recovered, or did she beg.

"I'm afraid, my friends, I am very much afraid indeed, that they will catch...

2.
A Font of Printers

A town's progress might be marked as substantial with the arrival of a newspaper. Now, 1855, William Green T'Vault, with "Messers Taylor and [Alex] Blakeley," hauled a printing press from a defunct paper at Scottsburg, in Douglas County's Umpqua Valley, to Jacksonville. They started the *Table Rock Sentinel.* This was the first newspaper in Southern Oregon. (Earlier, and for a very short time, the village had been called Table Rock for a nearby promontory.) T'Vault, the obvious leader and a lawyer, in time, bought out his partners. T'Vault was somewhat stern in his feelings about many things, especially Indians, having participated in the Rogue Indian War of 1853. Turnbull, writing in his book, *History of Oregon Newspapers,* commented about the military service recently experienced by T'Vault and noted that his record revealed he did his duty: "...with no great glory." *

On the top of the page of each issue of his paper, T'Vault displayed this statement:

INDEPENDENT ON ALL SUBJECTS;   DEVOTED TO THE BEST INTERESTS
OF SOUTHERN OREGON

He had a lively paper. He republished articles from papers in San Francisco, Hong Kong, the Puget Sound region, as well as new material picked up from travelers. He ran advertising including his own:

| W. G. T'Vault, Attorney and Counselor at Law |

---

* T'Vault was a man of prominence and held important positions in early Oregon government. These included being Oregon's Postmaster General as well as editor of Oregon's first newspaper, *Oregon Spectator* in Oregon City. For details refer to *Oregon City (By Way of the Barlow Road) At the End of the National Historic Oregon Trail.* See bibliography.

Walling wrote:

T'Vault was a man of ability and force of character, compensating for lack of culture by force of will, uncompromising in his animosities, but fair to his friends.

He had been in charge of a small band of volunteers during the Indian War. While on an overland march through Douglas County, he chose a place for an overnight camp against the advice of one of his men. Earlier, the man had been involved in an Indian attack at this very place and told T'Vault not to camp there. T'Vault, being "Colonel" and assertively exhibiting his power as commander, decided to camp at the site anyway. During the night the little group was furiously attacked while they slept, nearly all being wounded or killed. T'Vault escaped through the brush unhurt but was obviously gun-shy of Indians ever afterward.

There was a farmer by name of John Beeson who had a spread near the present City of Talent. Beeson was very disturbed at what he called the barbaric treatment the Indians were receiving at the hands of some of the settlers and said so. Beeson was frequently on business in "J'ville" with his son, Welborn, and while there, the elder Beeson spoke to all who would listen about Indian rights. After many corner speeches, along with Beeson-written articles about brutality to Indians which T'Vault discovered were being printed in San Francisco papers, T'Vault, along with several others, called an "indignation meeting" in Beeson's neighborhood. In short, John Beeson was threatened to where he feared for his life. Therefore, late one night, he abandoned his wife, son, and farm to flee the country.*

T'Vault saw to it that the so-called community feelings against Beeson for his stand with the Indians, received "Page 1" space in the *Table Rock Sentinel.*

Over the next several years, the paper T'Vault started changed names, partners and owners several times. In 1859 it became *Oregon Sentinel.* The paper had been intensely Democrat and at times so radical that citizens loyal to the Union refused to buy or read it. Accordingly, the paper's financial matters became

---

* The story appears in the book *The Plea for the Indian by John Beeson — Oregon's First Civil-Rights Advocate.* Introduction by Bert Webber, M.L.S. Here are the colorful details of Beeson's many years fighting for Indian rights. See Bibliography.

untenable thus the publisher closed shop in 1861.

Turnbull wrote of the many papers in town:

Jacksonville, interesting old southern Oregon town, is a focal point in early Oregon journalism.

On a nice typically hot summer day, August 1, 1857, following a notion that if a community would support one paper two would be better, two men started the *Jacksonville Herald.* It was published by William J. Beggs and B. J. Burns.

The Beggs and Burns team listed their major equipment as

1 Imperial No. 3 Washington press	4 wood galleys
1 rolling frame	3 composing sticks
2 double chases pair of cases (type)	1 lead cutter
5 job cases (type)	1 large font *Bourgeoise* type
1 hand roller frame	1 large font *Brevier* type
4 brass proof galleys	8 fonts *English* type
	6 printer's candlesticks

The *Herald* underwent more changes than did the *Sentinel* and lasted a very short time. When it was time to sell out, the inventory reported here, plus miscellaneous plunder, was listed at $1,400.00.

When the *Sentinel* folded, its plant was used by Messers O'Meara and Pomeroy to start the *Southern Oregon Gazette.* One historian, Turnbull, reported that the *Gazette's* editorial policy was so disloyal to the government that very shortly it was refused entry into the United States Mail. Thus, the *Gazette* died quickly for the post office was the major manner of circulation.

The next paper for Jacksonville was the *Civilian,* also Democrat but of a much milder form. Readers had been burned by Democrat editors so the *Civilian* was unpopular from the start and also died. In 1863, T'Vault took possession of the *Civilian* and changed it to the *Intelligencer,* but that paper also didn't pay so T'Vault quit the publishing business and gave all of his time to his lawyering.

The *Oregon Reporter* arose from the ashes of its predecessors in January 1865, but that too failed within a year. Under new ownership, the paper hit the streets in 1867 with its new name, *Southern Oregon Press.* This lasted several months, to be followed by the *Reveille* which also had a short stand. In 1869 the

California Street 1982. Building on right is original office of T'Vault's *Table Rock Sentinel*.

Democratic News came out under the leadership of P. D. Hull and Charles Nickell. The paper was just getting its feet on the ground when the plant burned in the fire of 1872. As quickly as new money was available, the *Democratic Times* was started by Nickell and survived to the turn of the century when it was consolidated with the *Southern Oregonian.* One of the type cases used by the *Times* ended up in the composing room of the Medford *Mail Tribune,* the case having originally been T'Vault's on his *Table Rock Sentinel.*

In 1906, a weekly, the *Post,* came along. This paper appeared at a time of less national controversy and lasted many years. There is mention of another paper, the *Miner,* in 1933, in Francis D. Haines Jr.'s book, *Jacksonville; Biography of a Gold Camp.*

For a short time the *Weekly Independent* was published, then there was the *Sentinel-American* in 1963.

In the 1980's, the Jacksonville *Nugget,* a weekly, appeared with local news. In the 1990's, the *Jacksonville Review,* "a monthly community newspaper," arrived.

The major papers circulated in Jacksonville at this writing are the Medford *Mail Tribune,* a Portland paper, the *Oregonian,* and papers from San Francisco. □

3.
Steps Forward

For awhile, Jacksonville was the largest city in Oregon (Walling p. 342). There was express service, stage lines and mail. There were local merchants and a banker C. C. Beckman. In 1856, Beekman reported that the "diggins" yielded close to $1,500,000, the greatest haul for a single year during the approximately ten years the placer gold lasted in southwestern Oregon. After 1856, as this surface ore dwindled, it became necessary to employ heavy mining equipment to get to the gold. Experienced prospectors realized that easy-panning days had passed so they too –unless they turned to farming – passed from the scene.

*　　　　*　　　　*

The first Presbyterian missionary, Moses Williams, arrived in 1857 and preached his first sermon in a school near what was later to become the city of Ashland. Reverend Williams was commonly called "Father" because "he looked patriarchal and spoke like a prophet." He formally organized the first Presbyterian Church in Southern Oregon at Jacksonville that year. As the Presbyterians had not yet erected a building, the Methodists shared theirs and together they later formed The Union Sunday School. This cooperation continued until the Presbyterians opened their own building in 1881.

Williams, educated at Columbia University and Princeton Theological Seminary, was ordained for the Presbytery of Georgia in 1846. Although his home was in Ashland, he formed Presbyterian Churches in Jacksonville, Phoenix, Ashland, Medford and in Eagle Point. He probably preached more sermons, married more couples and presided at more funerals than any minister during his thirty years' residence in Jackson County.

Rev. Moses A. Williams, founding Presbyterian missionary-minister, later Superintendent of Jackson County Schools.

One of the best educated men in the area, he thought highly of public schools. Although he was a practicing clergy, he was elected County Superintendent of Schools. Williams divided the county into school districts which, for the most part, remain intact today. He strongly advocated Bible reading in the schools and there did not seem to be any open discontent about this. During official visits to schools as Superintendent, he gathered children about him and told Bible stories. "Father" Williams died in 1887 and was buried in Jacksonville's cemetery.

*   *   *

With more and more people settling in and around town, and with a strong influx of merchants representing all types of goods, the muddy trails (loosely called "streets"), had to be improved. In the early '60's, the town council decided to grade the streets. A major thoroughfare, the "stage road," went through Jacksonville from Rock Point on the Rogue River via Willow Springs (west of Central Point), then through Phoenix to Ashland, and on over the Siskiyou Mountains into California.

As we have seen, the nearest sea port was Crescent City about 100 miles away. The lonesome, winding trail over mountains and through deep valleys was a hard pull for any size team. Making the trips were swarthy mule skinners who exacted a goodly fee in exchange for their hard and often frustrating work.

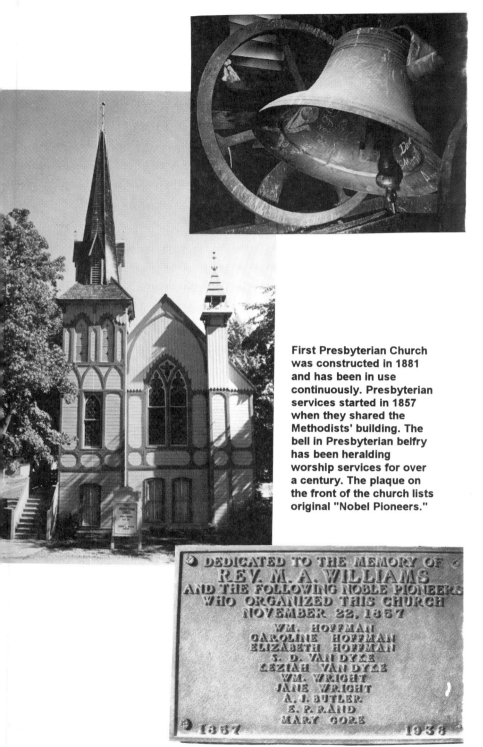

First Presbyterian Church was constructed in 1881 and has been in use continuously. Presbyterian services started in 1857 when they shared the Methodists' building. The bell in Presbyterian belfry has been heralding worship services for over a century. The plaque on the front of the church lists original "Nobel Pioneers."

DEDICATED TO THE MEMORY OF
REV. M. A. WILLIAMS
AND THE FOLLOWING NOBLE PIONEERS
WHO ORGANIZED THIS CHURCH
NOVEMBER 22, 1857

WM. HOFFMAN
CAROLINE HOFFMAN
ELIZABETH HOFFMAN
S. D. VAN DYKE
KEZIAH VAN DYKE
WM. WRIGHT
JANE WRIGHT
A. J. BUTLER
E. P. RAND
MARY GORE

1857   1938

A thriving village, Sailor Diggings (later Waldo), where sailors, who had jumped ship at Crescent City, had discovered gold in 1852, became a major stopping place. By the summer of 1860, a greatly improved wagon road was completed between Waldo and the coast. Freight wagons, sometimes with two heavily loaded trailers, pulled by 16 to 18 horses, hauling as much as thirty tons of goods, plodded along the road. To avoid head-on collisions on the narrower sections, bells were attached to the lead horses. It's been said that those people living along the road could identify a team before it came into sight by their different bell tones. The better road and easier travel lowered prices on goods destined for Jacksonville. Along with this improvement, the Mexican mule packers slowly went out of the packing business and left the scene. During this period, a twice-weekly stage coach carried passengers between the coast and Jacksonville, as well as express and plausibly mail.

*   *   *

R. Dugan was appointed Postmaster and opened the Post Office in Jacksonville on February 18, 1854. This was at a time when the Post Office Department was experiencing rapid expansion because of the influx of pioneers and gold-seekers in the west.For years, letters were sent to Post Offices the writers knew to be near where their emigrant family members and friends had settled. In the Bear Creek Valley, it was common for letters to turn up in any of several Post Offices where neighbors stopped on every trip to town, seeking mail for themselves as well as for friends. Before the publishing of the *Table Rock Sentinel,* the only newspapers in the area came as mail subscriptions from many of the settlers' old home towns in the east.

The California Stage Company, which had been operating from Portland through the Willamette Valley and on to Sacramento, made a stop in Jacksonville. In 1860, the firm was awarded a mail contract over this long route. Not very comfortable four-horse stage coaches became a daily sight in Jacksonville and shortened the arduous travel time. But the stages were usually overcrowded. Many tired and dusty passengers looked forward to a rest, usually overnight, in the hotels of "J'ville," Spartan as they were. □

St. Joseph's Roman Catholic Church was constructed in 1859.

4.
St. Joseph's Parish

As noted earlier, the Roman Catholics had explored Southern Oregon in 1853. Following this, the Diocese sent priests on field trips annually into the Jacksonville area to keep tab on the growing community. Archbishop Norbert Blanchet, of Oregon City, had once made the rough trip over the mountains in October of 1858. While in Jacksonville, he contracted for the construction of a church on a piece of donated land in the center of town. Based on a letter from Fr. Croke following an exploratory trip in 1854,

...the restless and reckless from everywhere seemed to be rushing 'from diggings to diggings and leading a life that is not far removed from barbarism.'

Thus the archbishop believed there was room in the town for a Roman Catholic presence.

Farnum wrote that Jacksonville's

weekly population of eight hundred, miners, packers, storekeepers and gamblers, swelled by the thousands on the Sabbath as men streamed in from the hills to dissipate their hoards [of gold dust] in horse racing, gambling, lawsuits, trading and the like.

(Left) Fr. J. T. Fierens, first resident priest in Jacksonville. (Right) Fr. Francis Xavier Blanchet, second resident priest, as seen through the 25 years he stayed. He was nephew of the Archbishop. Fr. Blanchet built strong Catholic membership in Jacksonville. He opened St. Mary's Academy.

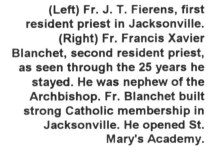

St. Mary's Academy in the early days. (Center) Fr. Blanchet in the church rose garden. Same view (bottom) in 1982. In mid-1930's, garden was torn out to make way for Depression-era gold mines.

Interior, St. Joseph's Catholic Church. Archbishop Francis Norbert Blanchet said Mass here in 1860.

Work started in 1859 on a Catholic Church after founding Father James Croke had collected "in cash $856" from miners and others as far as 65 miles away. He reported to Fr. Blanchet that his trip into the countryside was revealing as to just where the church-oriented Catholics were living – obviously not in Jacksonville.

[My trip] was very fortunate for otherwise I could scarcely collect only $30 in Jacksonville. They all promise and will give their names very readily to be paid at some future day, but names won't build a church.

Once construction started, Fr. Croke sent an enthusiastic letter to Father Blanchet. He wrote:

The church looks very high and when completed will be a neat building It will be 36 x 23 feet.

But he was a traveling missionary. He was not permanently assigned to Jacksonville so he left town to attend to priestly work in Yreka, California. On his return, he complained that after having been gone awhile,

I was surprised to find so little done to the church during my absence. The carpenters give excuses....

The first services were apparently held in 1859, then in 1860 Archbishop Blanchet visited Southern Oregon a second and last time offering Mass from the little church. By 1861, a parish priest had been appointed, Rev. Joseph. T. Fierens, who would reside in

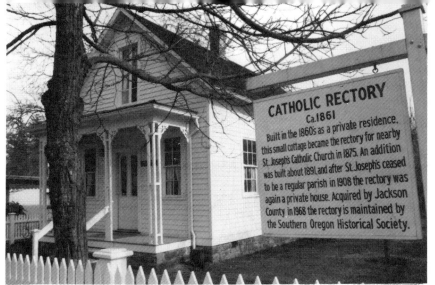

Jacksonville. A house was found near the church and arrangements were made to use it as a rectory. Fr. Fierens stayed until late November 1863 when he left for Portland. There he built a cathedral and served out the rest of his life.*

Fr. Fierens' replacement was the Rev. Francoise Xavior Blanchet, a nephew of the Archbishop. Under Fr. F. X. Blanchet's guidance, the parish grew and became consolidated.

In the meantime, as we have seen, the Methodists and Presbyterians were quite busy and had started The Union Sunday School. We also recall that Emma Royal held school classes. Seeing these, Fr. Blanchet was convinced that Catholic education was needed. He was successful in raising $2,139 in southern Oregon and adjacent California for a school so he wrote to the Mother Superior of the Sisters of the Holy Names of Jesus and Mary in Portland seeking teachers.

With the money, he bought some property and a piano and kept enough to pay for transportation of the nuns. Sisters Mary Febronia and Mary Zotiquet, with Sister Mary Delores, superior, arrived to teach in the school.

The school, to be called St. Mary's Academy, opened September 11, 1865 with 12 boarding and 33 day students. The school offered classes in art and music as well as the usual basic education. We note that photographer Peter Britt sent his

* Fr. Fierens, (1828-1893) a Belgian, became Vicar General at Portland and built The Cathedral of the Immaculate Conception of the Blessed Virgin – called St. Mary's Cathedral.

daughter as a boarding student to the Academy where the teaching was reported to be very strict. On one occasion, the students were quarantined during Christmas vacation because of measles. Miss Britt was determined to be with her family so she opened a window then slid down a balcony pole and went home.

The Academy started at 5th and D streets and was later moved to a location across the street from the Presbyterian Church.

Fr. Blanchet (b. July 22, 1835 - d. May 22, 1906) was well-schooled and took his responsibilities most seriously. He did everything in his power to promote and advance Catholicism in Jacksonville. His masses were well attended. His homilies were often aimed at fund raising for church related projects, or levied against specific groups such as the Masonic Lodge. He was often gone from Jacksonville since his many missions extended as far north as Corvallis, to Empire on Coos Bay and to Lakeview. During his sometimes lengthy absences, it was not always possible to have an assistant or bring in a temporary priest, thus his flock, unattended, sometimes wandered.

Following the smallpox epidemic, he became so ill from overwork that an emergency message was sent to a priest in Yreka to come to anoint Fr. Blanchet. This was done and, fortunately, he recovered. Fr. Blanchet was at St. Joseph's Parish for 25 years (1863-1888).

In 1875 he arranged to purchase the house, which had become a rectory, on a sheriffs sale.

Mission stations supervised by Fr. Blanchet included Ashland (1875) and Medford (1890). In 1912, with population trends reversed, the church became a mission of Medford then closed in 1940. After sixteen years, it was reopened again as a mission of Medford. Although the little building seats only 103, the building is, at this writing, comfortably full for Sunday Masses.

Over the next twelve years, according to official church records, nine priests were assigned to the parish. On July 10, 1889, the nuns operating St. Mary's Academy closed the school "because of a lack of 'spiritual succor,' the pastor often being on missionary trips for three weeks at a time." Also, the school building was badly in need of repairs which the Sisters were not

Interior of Catholic Rectory. The building is presently maintained by Southern Oregon Historical Society.

able to make. Many people in Jacksonville signed a petition that the school might be reopened, but the re-establishment did not happen until 1891. *□

---

* The Academy was moved to Medford in 1908. At that time, there were 126 students taught by six sisters. In 1949, Sacred heart Parish purchased the school from the Sisters of the Holy Names thus the school became a parish school. It was renamed St. Mary's School. By 1960 the school was divided into separate elementary and high schools. The lower school was renamed Sacred Heart School. The new high school took the name St. Mary's High School. In 1971, operating costs were so great for both schools that the Sacred Heart Parish Council voted to close the high school. However with community support, the high school remained open having been incorporated as an independent school.

A disastrous fire all but leveled the elementary school in 1987 but was rebuilt as a six-year school by moving 7th and 8th grades to the St. Mary's building. In 1992 the 6th grade was also moved thereby providing a three year middle school and a four year high school.

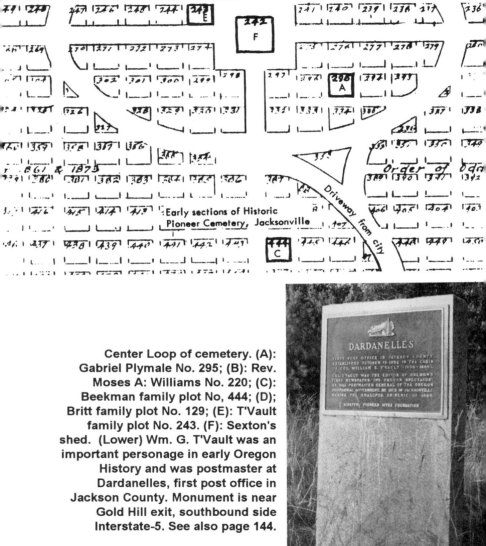

Early sections of Historic Pioneer Cemetery, Jacksonville

Order of Odd

Driveway from city

861 & 1875

Center Loop of cemetery. (A): Gabriel Plymale No. 295; (B): Rev. Moses A: Williams No. 220; (C): Beekman family plot No, 444; (D); Britt family plot No. 129; (E): T'Vault family plot No. 243. (F): Sexton's shed. (Lower) Wm. G. T'Vault was an important personage in early Oregon History and was postmaster at Dardanelles, first post office in Jackson County. Monument is near Gold Hill exit, southbound side Interstate-5. See also page 144.

44

5.
Epidemic

In late 1890, an alarm rang through the village when a case of smallpox was detected. The first report indicated the case to be merely chicken-pox so by the time a corrected diagnosis was made, the case was full blown. Those attending the victim, a half-breed Indian/white, had freely circulated throughout the town. The genesis of an epidemic had been spread and it was not long before a death was announced. Although attempts were made to cloak the death in secrecy with the burial taking place at night, there were blunders and almost immediately additional cases were identified.

A town-wide quarantine went into effect and word was spread throughout the Rogue Valley telling all others to stay away. Normal day-to-day activities in Jacksonville stopped. The school was closed. Church services were canceled. All public gatherings were discontinued. Just south of town, a "pest house" was set up to which the sick were taken and every possible care given. Despite the quarantine, word reached Jacksonville of two deaths by smallpox in another locality.

In Jacksonville, the disease spread like a blanket and so did panic. Vaccinations were given. Even with this precaution, many seemed unable to relax. Walling wrote:

Ministers fled in affright from paths of duty but in the darkest hours, the Catholic Priest [Fr. Blanchet] who himself had experienced the disease, together with the Catholic sisterhood, rendered valuable assistance. The contagion was not confined to any particular class. The widow of John Love, a lady of refinement and culture, was attacked and with her youngest son, was carried away. Her mother and the rest of her children were in the country and dared not approach her, and, when all was over, the unsightly corpse – all that remained of human beauty – was borne to the cemetery in a rough lumber-wagon without a single follower.

The first burial in the new cemetery was that of Gabriel Plymale in 1852. Regretably, over the years, many markers have been damaged by vandals.

(Top to bottom) Sexton's work shed in cemetery built about 1868 but recently restored. Storage vault under floor exhibited by sexton Wayne Maxon. Bodies were kept here before undertaking parlors had refrigeration. William G. T'Vault, a victim of the smallpox epidemic, is buried here.

Cemetery is picturesque – attracts thousands of visitors.

William Green T'Vault had led an active life in Oregon. At 63, he died of smallpox during this terrible epidemic. He was buried at midnight by Fr. Blanchet who had attended T'Vault's dying moments. T'Vault had become a Catholic only a few weeks earlier. Due to the risk, his many friends did not dare join the depressing walk up the hill to the cemetery. (T'Vault's grave and marker are easily located being near the sexton's shed.)

For about two months, the townspeople were in a state of confusion with death all around. Gradually the disease slackened then wore itself out but those who recovered would carry scars on their bodies for the rest of their lives. Jacksonville lost between forty and fifty of its people and in the small community their absence was notable.

One of the town's leading citizens, George Funk, died in a lonely cabin on the outskirts of town, cared for by members of the Odd Fellows Lodge. He was temporarily buried at the site as it was not considered wise to haul his body through town to the cemetery until some time later.

The people sought to end the pestilence by burning pitch-pine in the streets. This caused a layer of smoke to hang over the little town day and night to "purify the air." It gave off a ruddy glow that lighted the streets. Such was the custom of the day. The smoky atmosphere didn't improve breathing and the so-called "cure" turned out to be no cure at all.

The sisterhood from St. Joseph's Parish endeared themselves to the entire community of Jacksonville, having given tirelessly of their nursing skills to the many victims of the smallpox epidemic of 1869. □

6.
The Chinese

The Chinese were never well received in mining camps and the Jacksonville situation was no exception. Drunken whites harassed Chinese merely because they were "different." It was clearly evident that the Chinese miners worked harder and worked longer hours. They kept their gold and themselves within their own little corner of town and did not frequent the saloons. Jacksonville, really a shanty town, did not cover a great area, so although the Chinese kept to their own "quarter," they were not that much removed from everybody else.*

Whites paid lower wages to Chinese workers who were glad to have the jobs, most being the very hard, or "coolie" work as it was called denoting work done by a person of a lower class.

Many white miners were sloppy with their work. When they believed a claim was playing out they abandoned the area and moved on. Chinese miners leased these claims or often just moved in then worked these same areas over and over again getting gold until there was absolutely none left.

Passenger lists reveal the Oregon Stage Company brought a steady stream of Chinese from California to work the Southern Oregon gold mines. The records of Jackson County Mining

---

* The Chinese came to Oregon with the intention of working hard in the gold fields to earn money which they sent to their families in China. At such time as the work gave out, they planned to return to China. The majority did. Others, on leaving the gold mines, moved to Portland, Seattle or to San Francisco. For more information on the Chinese gold miners see the book *Gold Mining in Oregon – Past and Present*. See bibliography.

48

Claims shows that whites often sold their claims, which they believed to be worn out, to Chinese.

In an effort to control Chinese mining, pressure was brought on the Territorial Legislature to tax Chinese engaged in mining. The tax license was $2 *per month,* and all able-bodied Chinese who resided or remained in any mining town were regarded by law as "miners" unless directly engaged in some other business.*

When the constitution of Oregon was being debated, an entry for September 15, 1857 reads:

> If Chinese emigration continued to come into Jackson] County [it was] predicted that in five years no white man would inhabit it. White men could not compete with them – they work for $1.50 or $2.00 per day.
> —Carey, C. H. *The Oregon Constitution and Proceedings and Debates of the Constitutional Convention of 1857.* Salem. 1926 p. 361.

In Article XV, Sec. 8, is the stipulation

> No Chinaman [sic] not a resident of the state at the adoption of this constitution shall ever hold any real estate or mining claim or work any mining claim therein.

By the 1860's, the Chinese were still working so-called worn out claims. Their numbers were greatly diminished, but those who remained were methodical. If they hit a vein, they worked it until they got it all. In one instance, a group followed a minimal trail of gold by digging a ditch from Jacksonville all the way to a point near Gold Hill.

About the only time the Chinese stepped out into their own community was during the Chinese New Year. With the traditional Chinese Dragon leading a parade, these folks paraded in serpentine fashion around the town then back to their colony with most of the town's kids bringing up the end. The children were treated to Chinese "goodies" and everyone enjoyed themselves. A few days later, when activity was "normal," the kids who had been treated one day, were throwing rocks at their hosts the next.

Very few Chinese stayed in the county after the gold ran out, then these too eventually drifted away. □

---

* Laws of Oregon Territory, 8th Session 1856-57 p. 13. Readers may want to be aware that there were two major mining areas in Oregon. These were in southwestern Oregon of which Jacksonville was the principal community and in northeastern Oregon in which Baker City was the most populated town. –Ed.

Two of many historic houses in Jacksonville. (Top) Jeremiah Nunan house on Old State Road. It was ordered from a catalog in 1890. (Lower) Benjamin F. Dowell house, 1859 is across from supermarket.

7.
The United States Hotel and President Hayes

A place in history was assured the United States Hotel when President and Mrs. Rutherford Birchard Hayes, and party, stayed overnight on the 27th of September 1880. A member of the party was General William Tecumseh Sherman. The story, with a variety of spicy potpourri added during the century following, is a good one to review here.

The building was not yet ready for guests but last-minute fixings were added in an effort to make the President's visit comfortable. The history of the hotel is notable because of the building's enduring nature and the love held for it by many Jacksonvillians in addition to the fact that a President of the United States stayed there.

The United States Hotel, the second of that name, was constructed in 1880. It's most distinguished guests were President and Mrs. Rutherford B. Hayes.

A jolly but shrewd businesswoman, Màdame Jeanne deReboam, operated a boarding house in town during gold rush days. Later, she had a place she called the "Franco-American," which was also a boarding house. One rented a room for a period of time – normally longer than merely overnight – with breakfast and supper included in the bill. La Màdam´ was an extra-ordinarily good cook and had no trouble keeping her place full.

Down the street was the United States Hotel which pretty much catered to one-night visitors.

After the U. S. Hotel burned in one of several downtown area fires, the lot was deserted. Through a former owner, Louis Home, the Màdam´ bought the lot. But she was confronted with a challenge: How to get a building on it?

There happened to be a skilled builder in town who also owned the brick kiln, George W. Holt. And there are some who believe the following as fact, others prefer to call it "spicy-intrigue" to make a good story. Anyway – it is told that a business deal was struck between "Jeanne-baby" and Holt whereby she would share his bed and provide his board for the rest of his life if he would build a brick hotel for her. Further, the deed must state the

George W. Holt, a building contractor, was commissioned to build the hotel by Mádame Jeanne de Roboam (right). She became his wife as part of the "deal."

property would revert to her heirs on their deaths. (She had a son who wasn't known locally.) Holt agreed. They married of course, which was the fitting thing to do.

In March 1879 Holt went to work. That he was expert is attested by the fact the building still stands over 100 years later. Though there were periods where severe renovation was needed, it's still in use. He designed the entire structure. He hired some outside workers but he also spent many hours in actual construction. There was no hurry to get the job done so Holt took well over one year with it.

For a dance on the 4th of July 1880, the upstairs ballroom was opened but the whole building was really not yet finished. It would be February of 1881 before Màdam' Holt (nee deRoboam) was ready for any renters.

When the President's party showed up in the fall of 1880, as we have seen, the building was unequipped and not ready for anyone to live in. The President's group was traveling in two sections. The first passed through town without tarrying. The second group of eight was made up of the President and Mrs. Hayes; General Sherman; John W. Herron and wife; Mrs. John Mitchell; Dr. D. L. Huntington, all USA; (Col.) John Jameson.

Haines wrote of "a woman newspaper correspondent" who

53

U. S. Hotel in late 1880's. Men on balcony possibly members of Order of Red Men identified by cross-sash ornamentation. It was widely believed that gatherings of this size on balcony caused it to weaken, collapse.

accompanied the President. *

The group arrived in the evening to a welcoming committee of a small group of Republicans. As the mayor was a Democrat, he could hardly be expected to be seen. (Oregon was one of four states where the ballot had been contested. Hayes was declared winner by exactly one vote by a special election commission.)

The official greeting was a booming cannon and the brass band's appearance. As there was no advance warning of exactly when the group would arrive in town, all of the welcoming committee didn't make it. And of course, there had not been any earlier arrangements as to where this important party would spend the night. Màdam′ Holt was located and implored to find a way to put up everybody in her new hotel. No rooms were ready. There was no furniture. There were no bed sheets or blankets. And further, the paint was fresh and sticky.

* The Rutherford B. Hayes Library advised the authors that the so-called journalist was Laura Platt Mitchell – Mrs. John – a niece of the President. The librarian was insistent that Mrs. Mitchell was *not* a reporter. See bibliography for Haines' book.

54

Interior U. S. National Bank ground-floor of U. S. Hotel, is a full-service branch but decorated in 1880-style.

Recalling that the ballroom had been opened for the summer dance, it was dusted out and a reception and dinner was hastily planned. Even though it was already evening, the dinner would have to be stalled. The leading Republican, "Old Beek," turned out for the occasion and was pressed into being the welcoming speaker. In his book, Frank Haines wrote:

> This dinner featured First Lady Mrs. Hayes, known as 'Lemonade Lucy' for her prohibitionist activities. [She] turned her wine glass upside down as a gesture of refusal. The ladies were so charmed by this genuine bit of Washington etiquette, that it became a local fashion.

The next morning the visitors were up early and left town in their 3-team stage coach before most of the town knew they were gone. All kinds of stories have evolved since that less-than-24-hour visit of a President of the United States to Jacksonville, Oregon.

Probably the most quoted unprovable anecdote has to do with the bill for $100 for the group's dinner and lodging. On eyeballing the bill, General Sherman is supposed to have retorted, "My dear lady, I did not intend to buy your hotel" (But he paid the bill.)

Another story goes that Mr. President complained later about having been attacked by bedbugs. Mercy! But bugs in borrowed bedding, especially in 1880 Jacksonville, could have happened.

The fact that a President of the nation stayed overnight in the

U. S. Hotel and Jacksonville Inn during summer 1993.

U. S. Hotel adds to the lore of the town although to this day no one knows which room he occupied or from where the bed-bugged-bedding had been borrowed.

Years later the grand old building was ordered closed by the State Fire Marshall. He declared the hotel no longer safe. For one thing, the roof had been mended and re-covered so many times that its weight was about to collapse into the ballroom below it. The town library, that had space in the hotel, was forced to move.

Eventually, the hotel was restored by activities of the Jacksonville Properties for Historic Preservation and the Lions Club. In summer, there have been special musical features of the Britt Music Festival in the ballroom.

The United States National Bank of Oregon's Jacksonville branch occupies part of the ground floor. The bank has taken great pains to furnish its office with fixtures fitting the early days. Many of these furnishings are authentic while some, needed to complete the office, are new but constructed to resemble original pieces. On some days, the bank employees dress in the costumes of the historical period. (And yes, there are some hand-cranked adding machines and old typewriters in view but a banker there shied away from saying these museum-piece office machines were ever used.) The bank's clock is an 1876 model located in Jacksonville. The green shades on the windows are true to the decor of early times. The roll-top desk near the Branch Manager's corner is 1860-period of oak and walnut.

In the lobby of the hotel is a glass showcase with relics of early banking. ☐

Peter Britt, Oregon's first photographer. He was the first to photograph Crater Lake.

8.
The Photographer

There is little doubt that a locality will be remembered in later years if, during its forming years, the town was lucky enough to have had a photographer. Jacksonville is unique in this respect for in the 1850's, it was one of very few western communities with an expert resident photographer.

Peter Britt was a Swiss who came to America sometime

The Britt house and garden with daughter Mollie seated.

before 1845. The family settled in Illinois. In 1852, with two others, Peter traveled to Portland, then a frontier town. He was 33. He decided to head south with a yoke of oxen, a two-wheeled cart and a mule. He spent many days looking around the Willamette Valley but continued across the Calapooya Mountains into Southern Oregon. He came upon the gold mining village which was becoming Jacksonville. It was the 9th of November 1852. The village was merely a bunch of tents and a few log cabins.

Britt had trained as an artist: a painter of portraits. But in St. Louis, before heading west, he studied daguerreotyping as he believed Americans would accept and pay for photographs more readily than painted portraits. In Jacksonville, Britt took up a claim under the Donation Land Act on a hill at the southwest corner of the village. His first task was to construct a log cabin which would serve as home and as a work place, for he had

Britt lived to age 86, died in 1905. He used many cameras shown in exhibit in Jacksonville Museum.

carefully carried a small wooden box camera fitted with a Voightlander lens and some developing chemicals materials from St. Louis.

In his first months in the shanty town, he was not called on very often for photography so in the spring of the next year, he went into the pack train business. He moved freight from the wharf in Crescent City to Jacksonville. He pursued this work until 1858. Britt wanted to make pictures full time but he needed more equipment and a source for supplies. He went to San Francisco and brought everything he could think of with which to set up a formal studio.

On his return, he added a second story to the cabin and installed a skylight. His darkroom was also upstairs. Britt photographed people as they were. These included miners in rough clothing with pick and pan. Chinese he pictured in native dress. He did portraits of Indian maidens; soldiers; children; the businessmen of town. He also made photographs of family groups. He liked the out-of-doors so photographed buildings, parades, mountains, flowers, lakes and streams. He was the first to photograph Crater Lake (1874). When the National Park Superintendent learned of this, he made immediate inquiry about getting extra prints.

In 1860, Britt built the large two-story house which was a landmark in Jacksonville for decades. He added more rooms in 1880. But Britt had other interests too. Having come from an area in Europe known for its fine wine grapes, he obtained starts from California and in a few years operated one of the first commercial wineries in Oregon. He put up Claret, Muscatel and Zinfandel which he distributed at wholesale.

Britt, a true believer in the value of catalog buying, ordered seeds and then planted many of the valley's first apple and pear trees.

When he was 42, he married a childhood sweetheart Amalia Grob who had been widowed with a small son. Peter and Amalia had three children of their own: Emil (1862); Arnold who died as a baby; and Amalia (1864).

To commemorate the occasion of the birth of his son, Britt planted a sequoia on the north edge of the property. It still stands.

Outline of Britt's home now part of county park.

His wife watched her husband's growing success but died in 1871 leaving him to rear the family.

Peter Britt loved his children and loved beautiful things. He worked hard to develop a garden around the house which included a fountain and a small pool. The property commands a view over the town and valley with the Cascade Mountains in the distance.

His son, starting at an early age, helped his dad in the studio. After Britt died in 1905, at age 86, his children, who never married, continued to live at the family home. They took great pains to preserve his work for he was an artist who had gone through life with seeing eyes, and had recorded what he saw with exacting and patient work. His great collection of glass plate negatives illustrate the growth of the community both in buildings and people who lived there or passed that way.

Peter Britt was the first photographer in Oregon. His cameras and much of his equipment are displayed in the Jacksonville

Cemetery monument to Peter Britt

Museum where hundreds of his photographs are exhibited.

Peter Britt, his wife and their two children, are all buried in the family plot in the Jacksonville Cemetery.

Peter's property was originally some ninety acres. It was given to Southern Oregon State College with the understanding the house and antique furnishings would be cared for. A caretaker was hired to live in the house but, unfortunately, the house burned to the ground.

After the fire, the gardens were reclaimed with much volunteer labor until early in the 1970's, when efforts by members of the community persuaded the County to buy eleven acres which were the location of his barn, house, orchards and gardens. The $40,000 paid for these acres is used by Southern Oregon State College for loans to students. The money has turned over many times.

After securing the land, the Britt Association worked about

eight years to obtain funds to build the present pavilion. Donations from individuals and businesses, along with a federal grant, enabled the construction of the pavilion. The County financed the construction of rest rooms and adjacent service buildings.

The foundations of the Britt home were outlined and an attempt made to replace the gardens as they were when the home still stood, with a grant from Oregon's Bi-Centennial commission.

A path was built for pedestrians from the public parking area north of Highway No. 238 behind the telephone exchange building to what is today called the "Britt Grounds."

The pavilion, which stands where the Britt barn stood years ago, was designed then built to allow performers to project variations within a musical score to the hillside audience. Initially, audiences brought blankets and sat on the grass however weatherproof benches have recently been installed.

Irrigation, overhead lighting and access for the handicapped is now completed. Jackson County Parks Department assumes responsibility for the upkeep of the grounds. Each summer, the Peter Britt Gardens Music and Art Association Festival presents summer concerts under the stars on this original Donation Land Claim. (See the chapter "Music Under the Stars.") □

Jacksonville Carriage Service's tours provides touch of nostalgia in Jacksonville...Antique Town in a Modern Age.

Cornelius C. Beekman at counter of his bank. He never modernized its interior which can still be seen today.

9.
The Banker

No name was better known in Southern Oregon banking circles than that of Cornelius C. Beekman and the Beekman Bank in Jacksonville.

He was a transplanted boy from New York City. He had been born on a very cold January 27th in 1828. He went to the common schools in the city and had trained as a carpenter. He was just 22 when he sailed to San Francisco, via Panama, then proceeded, with other gold seekers, to the Yreka area where he prospected for three years.

In 1853, he took a job with Cram, Rogers & Company, a branch of Adams & Company, express agents, in San Francisco

North side of California Street in 1993. Jacksonville Bakery on left, Wells Fargo Office/Beekman Bank at far right.

and Portland. He was regularly sent as messenger from Jacksonville over the lonely mountains to Crescent City carrying letters, papers and thousands of dollars in gold dust. In all the troubled times, the young fellow was never molested, although generally traveling alone and at night. In 1856, his employer went bankrupt and "Beek," as his friends called him, lost his job. Unperturbed and a self-starter, he went into the messenger business for himself, continuing the same routine. He rode at night, as mentioned, often changing his route. When a good stage road was completed over the Siskiyous between Yreka and Jacksonville, he was in the right place at the right time for Wells Fargo needed someone with experience to represent them at Jacksonville. Beekman accepted the post and kept it for many years.

In 1857, he opened a bank which he operated with extreme conservatism. He bought gold dust at discount directly from miners and transported it out of town. His profits were high and this venture guaranteed him a small fortune from the start. His bank was considered one of the richest banking houses in all the Northwest. For some years, after he took a partner, Thomas Reams, the bank was called "The Beekman and Reams Bank." When Reams died in 1900, Beekman continued alone. Of interest, is that Beekman did not pay any interest on deposits and when somebody wanted to borrow money, Beekman, if he approved of

Cornelius C. Beekman, messenger, Agent of Wells, Fargo & Co., Banker, Politician, Philanthropist.

the loan, provided his own money – never the bank's. *

As a financier and man of considerable ability, Beekman was repeatedly elected one of the town's trustees and for several terms was the elected Mayor of Jacksonville. For nine years he was President of the School Board and it was mainly through his efforts that the large brick school building, on the eastern edge of town, was built in 1908. His concern for educational advancement of the town's youngsters took a high priority in his life.

Beekman had interests in other fields as well. He was one of the founders of the Jackson County Land Association, that organization controlling large tracts of the county's land.

Of course a man of this ability would become involved in politics away from the homestead. We find Beekman, in 1878,

---

* The fact that Beekman did not pay interest and loaned his own money is an argument the U. S. National Bank of Oregon has used for years in trying to establish their fore-runner, Ladd & Tilton Bank, was the first bank in Oregon. But L&T did not come about until two years after Beekman opened his door. See bibliography for Adam Richter's book.

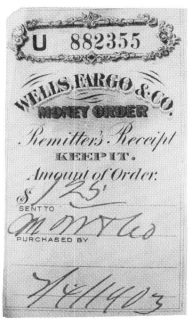

Receipt given customer for
Wells, Fargo & Co. Money Order
on Feb. 4, 1903.

being placed in nomination for Governor of Oregon on the
Republican ticket. It was a wildly contested campaign and when
the votes were in, "Beek" lost by only *forty-nine votes!*

The philosophy of Cornelius C. Beekman

**Let every man be occupied, and occupied in
the highest employment of which his nature
is capable, and die with the consciousness
that he had done his best.**

—borrowed from Sydney Smith

Beekman married Julia Hoffman, the daughter of the County
Auditor. They had two children, Benjamin B., an attorney, and a
daughter Caroline.

Beekman was, for twelve years, the Master of Warren Lodge
No. 10, A. F. & .A. M.*

As mentioned, Beek's bank was "different" in the manner it
held people's money. While many members of the community
were glad to have Beekman's banking services, decades later he
had a learned detractor. "In reality," opined Adam Richter in
1967, "Mr. Beekman directed a village safety deposit box and

---

*For details of some of Beekman's lodge activity, see the book, *The Lodge,
Jacksonville Masonic Fraternities.* See bibliography.

transported letters and other valuables." In seeming amazement Richter declared, "Moreover, [Beekman] never charged anything for the bank's service"!

Beekman developed a fortune by loaning his own money and collecting a good interest, but never by oppressing the poor or by taking advantage of the necessities of his fellows. During his early business as a messenger, he carried letters for $1 each before the Post Office opened in Jackson County.

Beekman decided to close business after 55 years. On August 13, 1912, he told the public he wanted to retire and would pay off all depositors. Considering that The Beekman Bank was the pioneer bank in the County, this caused quite a stir. But "Old Beek" was getting along in years.

The retirement of the bank's business went forth with assertiveness, but Beekman did not live to see his institution finally closed. He died on February 22, 1915, at age 87. (Beekman, his wife and their children are all buried in the Jacksonville Cemetery.) The final closing of the bank was completed by May 1, 1915.

Visitors to Jacksonville can view the banking office just as it was abandoned in 1915 at the corner of 3rd and California Streets. Under the control of the Southern Oregon Historical Society, a large glass has been installed so viewers can see the office and its turn-of-the-century equipment from the street. In addition, there are two Beekman "houses," both on California Street. An early residence is on the northwest corner of 6th and California Streets and is known as the "Minerva Armstrong House." Mr. and Mrs. Beekman lived there right after their marriage. The second house, known as "The Beekman House," is a little east of the Presbyterian Church, on the south side of California Street. Both houses are maintained by the Historical Society. The Beekman House is open for visitors in summer and other times by arrangement.

*　　　*　　　*

It must be acknowledge that "Old Beek" had some competition in the banking business starting in 1907. The Bank of Jacksonville was capitalized at $25,000 and experienced a period

U. S. Hotel (left) with Jacksonville Inn (right). The Inn offers 8 rooms, all furnished with antiques.

of growth right from the start. Part, possibly, because not everyone in town liked to do business with Beekman. But about two years later, the new bank experienced a sharp decline in deposits then a rapid recovery. This was followed in 1918 with another decline and the capital investment was reduced to only $10,000. Another binge of business brought the capital account to $15,000 but then trouble of a nature newspaper reporters love to report came to light.

In short, the Bank of Jacksonville was ordered closed by the State Banking Department on August 11, 1920. In the trial that followed, several officers of the bank were found "wanting" as well as two customers. Four men were sent to the State Penitentiary for their parts in the mishandling of funds. The liquidation of the Bank of Jacksonville was one of the most expensive undertakings of the State Banking Department and required only three months short of ten years to complete.

Of great concern was the fact that the Jackson County Treasurer had deposited county funds in the bank in the due course of business. The loss to the county as a result of the bank's failure was about $107,000.

The Bank of Jacksonville's closure left the town without a bank until 1965, when the United States National Bank of Oregon opened its Jacksonville Branch in the U. S. Hotel Building. In 1976, the Jackson County Federal Savings and Loan Association constructed a building, compatible with the neighborhood, on the corner of 4th and California Streets. □

(Top) North side of California Street in Jacksonville Historic District. (Lower) there are numerous eating places in Jacksonville, including this one where summer guests can dine on the lawn.

10.
Jacksonville Wanted A Railroad

The matter of having a railroad as well as a telegraph in the valley had been debated for years but with little result. But plans for a telegraph line between Portland and Yreka went ahead after meetings in Jacksonville in October 1861. Fund raisers made the rounds in the spring of 1863 and work started shortly thereafter. The line was a tough job to install, due to the wild terrain of the Siskiyous, nevertheless, good progress was made and the first message was tapped out on January 23, 1864.

Initially, the plan for a transcontinental railroad was put on "hold" during the Civil War. But by 1863, the outlook for the cross-country rail service was becoming quite promising so Jacksonville's promoters decided on a project that would bring a train through Jackson County. Subscriptions were accepted for money as well as merchandise to help with costs which would arise with a route survey. The first survey started in the Sacramento Valley, near Marysville, at that time the northern terminal of the Central Pacific. The immediate plan was to extend that line to the Oregon border. The plan also called for a railway to be built in Oregon to join with the track in California. Although the money and goods collected didn't go very far, other interests stepped in each seeking a piece of the action.

By late summer of 1864, a survey in Oregon was finished to the Columbia River and the results were put before the Oregon Legislature. Result: The California and Columbia River Railroad Company was incorporated. Joseph Gaston, a lawyer and journalist, envisioning a great future for the railroad, took an active part in a long and heated controversy over which route the rails should follow. While this delayed construction, Jacksonville continued to flourish as the principal city of Southern Oregon even though the

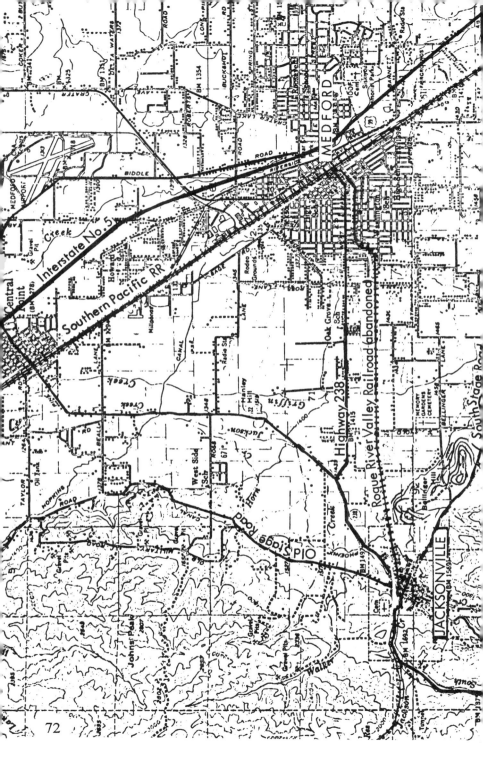

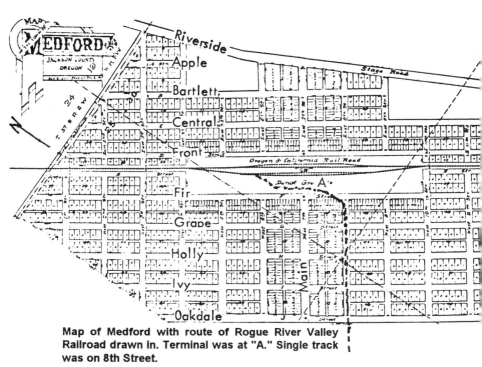

Map of Medford with route of Rogue River Valley Railroad drawn in. Terminal was at "A." Single track was on 8th Street.

miners had mostly moved on. After much turmoil in the courts over routes and grants, the Oregon and California Railway Company (O&C) was awarded a contact. Work progressed up the Willamette Valley to Eugene where serious debates over routes were rekindled. The choices appeared to be:

1. Would the route miss the Rogue Valley by crossing the Willamette Pass and enter California through Klamath County?

2. Would the right-of-way pass through Roseburg and the Rogue Valley then over the Siskiyous to the state line?

It was largely through the efforts of U. S. Senator George H. Williams (R-Oregon 1865-1871) that the route was decided in favor of the Rogue Valley.*

---

*Arguments were clear that the Willamette Pass route would not go through any communities other than Linkville (later re-named Klamath Falls) but the Siskiyou route would pass through North Canyonville, Roseburg, Phoenix and Ashland Mills before crossing into California. Further, the Siskiyou route was the earlier recommendation of the U. S. Army Corps of Topographical Engineers following their expedition of exploration of 1855. Historians have questioned the need for the survey of 1863-1864 in Oregon because of the pre-existence of the very thorough earlier survey by the Army Engineers which the builders generally followed anyway. Note that the route did not mention Jacksonville.

But the construction stopped at Roseburg without further progress for nearly ten years!

There was never a question in anyone's mind that the track, when work resumed, would pass through Jacksonville for Jacksonville was the largest city in Southern Oregon and was the county seat. Several ideas were discussed in town to further the stalled construction, one of which was the formation of the Humboldt Branch Railroad. This venture, the planners believed, would construct the line through the valley. But the scheme died.

Finally, when the Central Pacific decided to build their line northward in the Sacramento Valley, work again commenced at Roseburg. The people of Jacksonville followed progress of the work vividly. Word got out that the design engineers wanted to build in a straight line, after the track crossed the Rogue River, to a point near Ashland. Still, Jacksonville businessmen and residents were of a common mind: "The rails will come through our town."

When crews staked the line from Central Point to Phoenix, then on to Ashland Mills, which would be the division point at the base of the mountains, Jacksonville boosters were shocked into realization that their town was going to be left right where it was – five miles west of the line!

A local group wanted to bribe the railroad so somebody passed the word that the town needed to donate a station and yard site and hand over $25,000 cash, and the track would be routed their way.

Was it a sound idea?

Did anyone have any money?

Would Beekman's bank loan the money?

Answers: No, no, and no!

When it comes to building a railroad, the matter of who owns the land it will run on must be considered. Some Jacksonville property owners had planned on making a killing when they sold rights-of-way for the track. At least one did, but as we will see it was not in Jacksonville.

One night, several of the railroaders roomed at the cross-roads-village that eventually became the town of Central Point. This is about six miles northeast of Jacksonville. While there, the officials talked to the locals suggesting they put up money and land for switching tracks and a station. For some unrecorded reason, the proposition was not well accepted by the listeners. Folklore tells us that these locals told the money-hungry railroad men to "buzz off"!*

In retaliation, the design engineers decided to but their switch-yard a few miles south, in the middle of the Agate Desert and build a town around the station. This would draw trade away from Central Point.

It happened that some land in the center of the valley was owned by four men, one of whom was Beekman. They pooled their interests and platted a town site. They donated 240 acres to the engineer in charge of the O & C survey, then donated an extra twenty acres to the railroad for a station and switching yards – plus every other block within the town site. In all, the railroad received 41 blocks of the new "city." Many people in Jacksonville thought they saw a connection. Some believed that Beekman wouldn't loan money to bring the track to Jacksonville because if he did, he wouldn't be able to develop his land at trackside of the railroad. With a deal as good as this, why should a railroad detour its tracks via Jacksonville?

But there were other considerations that ruled out Jackson-ville. There's certainly no question that the most economical route over which to lay rails is in a straight line, especially when there are productive farms on both sides of that straight line. The O & C was also running short on money.

While it would be polite of the railroad to jog the tracks in the direction of Jacksonville, the town had no economic base from which to generate freight revenue. In addition, the entire route from the Rogue River all the way to the California line was up-grade, so why huff and puff by way of Jacksonville, which would deviate from the straight-line engineering principals, when there was no business to be gained?

Thus, observers have noted, the railroad never seriously plan-ned to pass through Jacksonville all the way back to the earliest surveying stages. Could it have been that the surveyors of 1863-

* Had the people at Central Point realized that the hand-outs the railroaders wanted would have, over the few years, put Central Point on the map in such a way that in all probability Medford would never have come into existence. —Ed.

Porter locomotive with combination passenger and Express car in Jacksonville.

1864 who had presented their recommendations to the Oregon Legislature knew full-well of the factors and felt they had some kind of a mandate to write Jacksonville into the plan?

Storekeepers in Jacksonville were getting nervous about construction at the new town. Some told customers the buildings were merely warehouses to transfer goods from the railroad to "J'ville." After all, Jacksonville *was* the county seat and as such, is the center of county operations. The new court house would be built the next year in Jacksonville and that alone meant stability they truly believed.

Meanwhile, and very quietly, some merchants prepared to move to the new town. Medford, as the town was to be called, was founded – or platted – during December 1883. It was a little over one year later, February 24, 1885 to be exact, when the Governor, Z. F. Moody signed the bill incorporating the City of Medford. On March 11 of the same year, the articles of incorporation were adopted locally.

Jacksonville began to feel it was slipping in importance when word first got out that the railroad would miss the town. Many shook their heads in wonder as to their future as Medford, that upstart railroad town to the east, became a reality. But "li'l ole 'J'ville'" would survive as a one-industry town – the county seat –

Arrival of locomotive, on a flat car, in Medford.

another 44 years.

When the politicians started to promote the removal of the county seat to Medford in the 1920's, Jacksonville's future appeared pretty dark. As one wag put it: "The town's future took on the look of a freight train roaring down hill with no brakes."

*   *   *

Even though the Oregon & California Railroad would never touch Jacksonville, interests in town wanted a railroad so much, they put their possibility thinking together and decided to build one of their own. Feelings ran high that with a short line to Medford, freight and passengers by rail would keep Jacksonville alive. It was a fight for survival in the minds of many, as Medford was growing, just a few miles to the east, as an unwelcome weed.

Ashland, never before of much concern to Jacksonvillians because of the distance, suddenly seemed much closer. It was the division point on the O & C Railroad folks were swelling the town whose population now topped Jacksonville's. In addition, there was an uncomfortable situation developing just six miles northeast: That village that became the city of Central Point moved itself a tad to the west to be alongside the track, had nearly

77

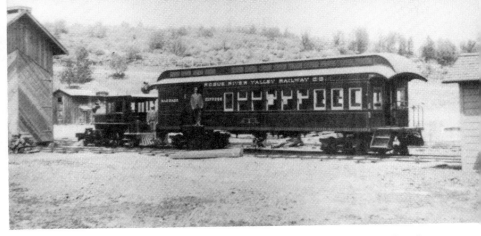

One-car train of the Rogue River Valley railroad standing in Jacksonville yard. The engine was under-powered for the task, had to be replaced with larger locomotive.

doubled in size and now straddled the rails. (Central Point got its name because two pioneer wagon roads intersected there, which is near the center of the valley.)

In Jacksonville, meetings were held and often became heated as committees pondered how to get, and where to seek a right-of-way between Jacksonville and Medford. A railroad would have to hire people for construction as well as for operation and this meant money would flow to Jacksonville, they reasoned. With this spark, even Medford became involved. People in both towns pledged a bonus of $20,000 to get a railroad out of the planning stages and into reality.

The first official effort was the incorporation of the Medford and Jacksonville Railway Company in mid-January 1890. This operation was to choose depot sites and prepare final surveys. There was a deadline just less than one year away. A train had to actually operate on the line if the bonus was to be paid. There was lots of pressure to get track down and find people to run it. But it is one thing to envision a system on paper and another to order, receive and install ties and rails, buy an engine and cars, have everything shipped and get a train to run. Time waits for no one.

With less than a month before the construction contract expired, rails had not been delivered let alone placed. The contractor left the job. To believe such a project could have been completed within the time allotted seems, with advantages of 20-

20 hindsight, to have been ill-conceived. There are no records found today for anyone to review as to the source or rail specifications. There is good reason to believe however, that a hardware store in Portland, Honeyman-DeHart & Company, that specialized in heavy metals, got the order. This dealer took delivery of second-hand, 36-pound rail which had come from England. They also scrounged up the Porter locomotive as part of the deal. As it turned out, the locomotive was the wrong size.

A new contractor was appointed and work progressed rapidly with new enthusiasm. What had been a job noted for delays, now went ahead with amazing speed. Final grading was completed just as Southern Pacific told the builders that a full train of flat cars carrying rail was due on the morrow.

Rails were nailed to ties in record time.

Fully aware they had no rolling stock, the contractor borrowed or leased an engine and car from Union Pacific. As there was still ill-feeling against the mainline firm for not routing their track via Jacksonville, why rent from them? It was now the Southern Pacific to be reckoned with as O & C had gone bankrupt while trying to get over the Siskiyou Mountains.

The deadline of January 1, 1891, was at hand. It was a very cold, rainy day. The U. P. engine made steam and barely started to roll when the track slipped and the engineer found his mount parked firmly in the mud! There was no ballast (rock) yet poured to weight the ties in the soft, wet earth. The Union Pacific locomotive was far too heavy for 36-pound rail on non-ballasted ties.

Jacksonville's people were not dismayed for long. They were pleased with the progress of their contractor so granted a construction extension. About two weeks later, folks suddenly froze in their activities as a sudden shriek split the air – a train whistle. The sound was primrose. The first train hissed and chugged its way into town to the site where the depot had not yet been built. There was a celebration that day to rival the 4th-of-July!

The new line was greeted with enthusiasm both by Medfordites and Jacksonvillians. Just about everyone wanted to ride the train although regular service was not yet available. All trips were being done with borrowed equipment as the ordered engine and cars still hadn't arrived. Nevertheless, groups chartered the

View of Jacksonville business district and C Street, with train, from top of Courthouse in 1891.

train for special trips. It was announced that the ride to Medford was only twenty minutes but that twenty minutes was, for the people, excitement "first class."

There was concern, in official circles, about the west-bound trip to Jacksonville which took longer. It was a steady uphill pull; not that the grade was overly steep or mountainous, as some writers would have readers believe.

The Medford Bench Marker reads 1,383 feet elevation and Jacksonville's 1,569. This is only 186 feet in five miles and considered non-noticeable to the eye, except for a trifling increase for a very short distance at the Jacksonville city limit near the school. Nevertheless, it costs more fuel to puff a train up any grade than when a train goes down grade.

The Union Pacific engine was returned with the arrival of Locomotive No. 1, a Porter, 10-ton engine. And with its arrival also came a new challenge. The little engine, which is said to have been designed for use on a near-flat surface and without much of a load, was severely under-weight and under-powered for pulling

Steepest Grade on the S.P.

It was pointed out that the O & C went broke trying to complete their line over the Siskiyou Mountains. It will interest some to learn that from Ashland to Siskiyou summit by straight line is about 9 1/2 miles. By the track, 17 miles. The grade commences immediately on leaving Ashland but increases to 3.3 percent, the steepest on the entire S. P. system near the summit at which point a train, with helper-engines connected, has climbed about 2,178 feet elevation. Even with today's diesel locomotives, helpers are required.

a train up the slight grade into Jacksonville. There was no choice but to find another engine.

The new short line received the U. S. Mail contract between its two terminals. Editorials in the Jacksonville *Democrat Times* envisioned an extension to the coast and a line to Eagle Point thence into Central Oregon and of course, transcontinental.

About one month after the track was finished, a new corporation was formed for the purpose of operating a railroad between the towns and for two miles west of Jacksonville.

We recall there was a brick works west of town. Brick is heavy. The manufacturers looked to selling their output not only in Jacksonville but elsewhere so it didn't take much persuasion for the railroad to put in a spur to the plant. Also, up Jackson Creek a ways was plenty of rock which could be used for ballast hence the plan to run the track two miles beyond town. These were days when if rock was needed from the side of a hill, or from a creek bed or river bottom, it was mostly for the taking – no "permit" was required for no such thing existed.

But all this construction would be costly. Capital stock of $100,000 to be split into 1,000 shares was offered and bought by investors. The company took the name Rogue River Valley Railway Company (even though it operated from a point – Medford – on Bear Creek), and began regular service on Lincoln's birthday, February 12, 1891.

There would be two round trips each day. Jacksonville's depot was constructed at the corner of N. Oregon and "C" Streets.

The larger locomotive for the railroad could pull much heavier loads. The train shown with combination Express-baggage-passenger car in rear, instead of behind tender, which is normal, waits on C Street, Jacksonville, facing west just over the Depot switch. Flag on pole atop courthouse (right rear) orients location.

(Renovated a few years ago, the depot was raised from its old foundation, a new foundation built then turned to face a different direction. At this writing, the antique building serves as the Chamber of Commerce Information Office.)

Southern Pacific would earn extra profits if their loaded freight cars were used an extra few days on another railroad therefore, instead of having to unload a freight car in Medford, only to have the goods reloaded on a car of the shortline, it was suggested and agreed that a switch between the two firms' lines be installed. S. P. henceforth would just park a car with Jacksonville-bound freight on the Jacksonville siding then the local engine would hook up for the final leg of the haul. As it meant faster service for "J'ville" customers, and was appealing to both railroads, the deal was approved.

In April of 1891, the contractors declared their work finished. The line was formally inspected and accepted and Jacksonville's people were happy with the news, for at last they had their railroad.

Although many speeches were made and lots of meetings

The late M. Dale Newton, railroad historian and map maker, at restored R.R.V.R.R. depot. Building presently serves as Tourist Information Office of Chamber of Commerce.

held, promoters were never successful in extending the line to Eagle Point. *

The stockholders, who turned out to be more interested in construction than in the day-to-day operations, leased the railroad in October 1893 to W. S. Barnum who lived in Medford. The deal called for Barnum to operate the line for two months – just until the end of the year. Probably the most newsworthy item about this lease was that Barnum's 14-year-old son became what the press heralded as the youngest railroad conductor in the country.

The 1893 national financial panic hurt plans for any expansion, even additional cars, as new investors could not be found.

Ownership changed several times resulting in the construction firm that had finished the work having to operate it. The line was, regrettably, not profitable. The haul was too short and there was

---

* In 1905, ground was broken in Medford for the start of construction of the Medford & Crater Lake Railroad. But this was also unsuccessful and the rights were purchased for a new operation called The Pacific & Eastern Railroad. This group was successful because it was backed by outside money and the P & E operated for a number of years. See *Single-Track to Jacksonville.* See bibliography.

Track of Rogue River Valley Railroad extended about two miles west of town up Jackson Creek to rock quarry. When rock was needed, one helped himself – no permits required. When electrified in 1915, this extension was abandoned as the steam engines had been sold.

only one recognized stop enroute, Perrydale Avenue, about midway between the two terminals. And this stop was out in the country with very few close-by residences to be depended upon for tickets. There was never any freight for Perrydale. If there was a stop at all, it was just a quick passenger stop. What freight was hauled went west, up the fuel-consuming ever-so-slight grade into Jacksonville. The train generally went to Medford – down grade – empty of revenue producing freight. Jacksonville, as county seat, needed the passenger service of that there was no doubt. There were "commuters" so the railroad sold monthly booklets of "commute tickets," each ride rated at 20 cents.

As there was little provision for maintenance, the cars as well as the roadbed deteriorated which forced frequent shutdowns.

Both nature and people play tricks on railroads. The operation was, of necessity, low budgeted. When the engineer got a good head of steam up in Medford for the run west, he tried not to pile any more wood into the fire box than was absolutely necessary to get the train into Jacksonville. If there was a stop at Perrydale Avenue, this took most of the reserve steam to get the outfit rolling again.

R. R. V. TRAIN DELAYED

JACKSONVILLE- The Jacksonville-Medford jerk water met with the usual delay Thursday night, only this was more unusual, when the engineer-fireman-brakeman-president-machinist-conductor-section-officeboy-official started out with a gallon of water, and a few sticks of wood and a broken injector to make the round trip to Medford, he found that the S. P. passenger from Portland was late and there was not sufficient water in the boiler to make the round trip and wait on the late S. P. train, but nevertheless the start was attempted from Medford. After traveling about a mile the engineer noticed that the water was very low in the boiler and attempted to start the injector, but the old faithful injector worked as it had oft done before (worked the engineer.)

The engine was backed down, by gravity, to a residence, the fire pulled and the boiler filled by buckets. By this time the boiler was cold and several long minutes passed before the steam was raised. When the beautiful iron horse and palace car entered the city another unexcusable stop was made in front of the court house, and there the Rogue River Fast Mail stopped for the night for want of steam. Several passengers became disgusted with the thing and walked to this city.

A Trip to Jacksonville
By Grace Davis

I went to Jacksonville on a swift passenger train which has just commenced running lately. The train is a combination of an engine and one passenger coach, and sometimes a freight car.

On my way to Jacksonville I saw a great many things of interest, green fields and pastures, farms, houses, orchards and some very beautiful flowers.

Some of the people I saw were very good looking, and others were not. I also saw some Chinamen but they were not any different looking than they are here, because they all look alike. I went around the city awhile and then to the court house to hear a speech after which I got my dinner at a restaurant. I saw the jail, many large stores and several nice dwellings. For my part I like Medford the best of the two towns for the reasons that it is a larger place and is on the main railroad.

The train, on entering Jacksonville over that "trifle" of a grade near the school, frequently met with delays because boys will be boys. The rascals sometimes greased the rails then disappeared into the building to watch the engine's wheels spin on slick iron. The train would quickly lose its momentum – stop. The engineer would appear shortly with a bucket of sand which he spread on the track so the wheels would regain traction. There were occasions when cattle occupied the track stopping the train, once putting the engine in the shop following such an encounter.

The owners, based in Portland, tired of the novelty of railroad ownership which didn't bring any profits, wanted out. Barnum, who had run the line for a couple of months earlier, bought the entire works for a reported sum of only $12,000.

Train, with steam up, in Medford Depot, seems to be waiting for woman on board sidewalk.

Under Barnum's ownership, the road became mostly a family operation as his wife and sons were put to work. He hired few outsiders except for firemen. This "Mom and Pop" operation saw Mrs. Barnum as secretary, treasurer and business manager. The boys worked in the shop, handled what track repairs were required to keep the train on them and of course, one son was conductor. Dad was General Manager.

The Barnums' did their best to run the venture as a profit-making business, but without substantial freight and with dwindling passengers – automobiles had arrived – the future was not bright. Jacksonville was definitely not growing. In fact, it was the other way around. Medford quickly surpassed Jacksonville in population and in the number of business houses. The orchard industry, apples and pears mostly, was centered in the valley and 'J'ville" seemed miles away. People silently blamed all of the town's troubles on Southern Pacific for the "shortsightedness" in skipping Jacksonville. And for shame, there was the beginning of talk about moving the county seat.

Barnum's life was never easy. He was charged with blocking traffic in Medford by leaving his train unattended for hours. Others contended the coach was unsafe and they had to resort to umbrellas on rainy days as the roof leaked. And the car creaked

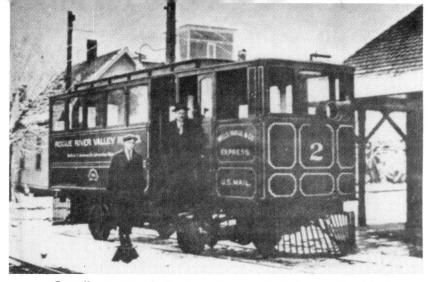

Gasoline-powered "train-car" operated at considerably lower cost than powering-up a steam engine. Unit was built in San Francisco. Riders complained it "jerked, squeaked" and made them seasick.

more than ever over the now deteriorating, uneven road bed.

When the all-surface road between Medford and Jacksonville opened, a jitney carried passengers for less fare than the railroad. Barnum was a fighter. He cut fares but it was expensive fighting. He purchased, on a build-to-order contract, a train-car. This was a combination freight and passenger unit powered with a gasoline engine. People charged that the thing "stunk, jerked" as it rolled along the track, and was not at all what they wanted. Their dreams, which were never defined, would never be realized.

Another challenge irked Barnum when in 1913, the Southern Oregon Traction Company formed for the purpose of installing electric interurban lines throughout the valley. Not that any such new transportation was needed, but that was the plan.

Barnum saw a way out of his headaches, so in 1915 he sold out to the interurban people for part cash and part mortgage *held by Barnum*! Here is where Barnum was shrewd. He really liked owning and running a railroad but he was out of cash. If he could sell out for a good sum of hard money and still hold the papers on the railroad, which was a proven loser, he'd get a rest, then eventually get the line back.

Of course the first thing the traction company did was to shut

"Auto-car" speeder of the R.R.V.R.R. standing in Jacksonville Depot. It was a fun-ride on the clickety-clackity car.

down the railroad and electrify it. Jacksonvillians believed this electrified line – trolley cars – would be the end of their problems with the railroad. It cost considerably less to run an overhead trolley car than to generate steam every time a train had to move.

A car was bought in Cleveland, Ohio from the transit system there and hauled to Medford on a flatcar. But "mass transit" developers failed to recognize the potential drain from their enterprise by automobiles which were increasing in surprising numbers. The cost of electrification was never recovered. In short order, as Barnum expected, the interurban people wanted out. Barnum got his line back in default but grossly improved. A few years later Barnum sold it again. Same deal: Cash, and mortgage which he held. Then he got it back again!

Somewhere along the years, not pertinent to this story, tracks were laid in Medford streets for local streetcar service there. A rare photo shows Barnum's steam engine and work car in the middle of a down town Medford street with crews digging up the street a few feet in front of the locomotive, laying ties and rails, then the work train proceeding a few more feet where the operations were repeated.

Medford had streetcar service for a short time but it, too, ran into money shortage. And some people complained about having

The Southern Oregon Traction Company ran trolley cars in down-town Medford and eventually extended to Jacksonville after the steam railroad was electrified. Full details are in *Single Track to Jacksonville, The Rogue River Valley Rail Road and the Southern Oregon Traction Company.* See bibliography.

to change cars from east Medford to the car that ran on the Jacksonville line. With all kinds of challenges, some with the streetcar car itself, a connecting switch was installed between the two companies' tracks. For awhile, the little single-truck car that had run on the Medford streets offered through service to Jacksonville. Every time some new sort of improvement was announced, Jacksonville's people cheered. But it all came crashing down when the power station serving the line burned.

By now it was summer of 1922. A couple of years later, when another prospective buyer came to town, a special hookup was made from the local power company for a demonstration ride from Medford to Jacksonville and back. This must have been quite a ride. The rails were overgrown with weeds and the corroded overhead wire shot sparks as the trolley wheel rolled along it. Because the track had settled, the few passengers received a swaying, seasick ride. The deal fell through.

In 1925, Barnum felt he'd had enough. He decided to pull up the track and sell out for scrap. But law suits stopped his tearing up city streets. Finally in 1925, the City of Medford, which very much wanted to rid its streets of the old rails, bought the entire line to the Jacksonville city limits. The city pulled up some rail but asphalted over much more.

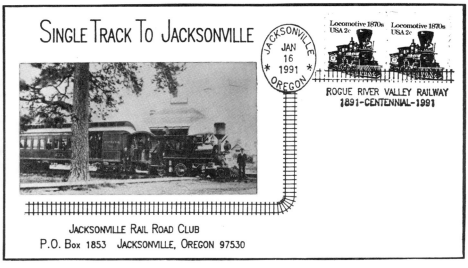

Souvenir cover (envelope) with special Jacksonville postmark issued on day the book about the railroad was published.

Medford did not sell all the rails. At the present time one can drive through the streets in southwest Medford, in the area where the tracks were, and one will still see rail but not in it's usual position in the streets. Several dozens of corner street name signs are held aloft on the ends of sections of railroad rail that now serve as poles.

At the present time, when street repairs are necessary, is not uncommon for workers to hit old rail much to the amazement of young-age TV reporters most of whom cannot believe that at one time there were trolley cars on Medford and Jacksonville streets.

In Jacksonville, the track was mostly left in the pavement from near the depot on "C" Street to 5th Street at the southwest corner of the museum. The track was asphalted over but at this writing, the thin layer of the pavement has worn off a short section of track exposing it to view. "Ah, ha" exclaim historians! But will the city cover it with street improvement projects in future?

*   *   *

The little locomotive, old No. 1, rusty and abandoned, went to a logging operation near Cottage Grove, Oregon, where it hauled short trains of logs on reasonably flat land. Still later, abandoned again, it was purchased by a woman as a gift to her husband who

Historic track emerges from pavement on C Street near museum. This and depot are only remnants remaining of railroad in Jacksonville.

was a steam locomotive enthusiast. The engine was shipped to California on a flatbed truck where it was restored, with some modification, as best as possible. It was eventually bought by a firm that rents several of its locomotives and trains for use, on its track, by professional movie makers. It is reported that the Porter, Jacksonville's original locomotive, is for sale. Jacksonville's tourist boosters look to the day when they might acquire the little locomotive and bring it home.* □

---

* Readers who are railroad enthusiasts will want to get the book *Single Track to Jacksonville, The Rogue River Valley Railway and The Southern Oregon Traction Company – An Oregon Documentary*. See Bibliography.

City Hall was built on lot where earlier had been the first brick building in town. That building burned in 1874. The present use of the old City Hall is for Municipal Court and public meetings.

11.
Telephones in Jacksonville

The date of exactly when the first telephones were used in Jacksonville is elusive but by 1878, people could talk on "wires" between Jacksonville and Yreka. A writer declared it was "undignified" to talk to an invisible listener. Telephones in rural areas were slow in being adopted primarily because of two factors. One was the high cost of planting poles and stringing wires over large areas. The second was the low revenue potential due to sparse populations. U. S. West Communications reports that the first local-use telephone in Jacksonville was in 1890. In 1898 the Sunset Telephone Company was in business and in the 1899 telephone directory for the county, there were only four subscribers in Jacksonville. These were:

Line No. 12   George Hines Boarding House
Line No. 13   T. J. Kinney Hardware and Grocery Store
Line No. 14   S. P. Roboam, United States Hotel
Line No. 15   John S. Miller, Hardware Store

In Medford, there were 16 lines.

The Home Telephone Company ran the small system starting in 1910 but sold to Pacific Telephone and Telegraph Company in 1935. This became Pacific Northwest Bell in 1961 then U. S. West in 1984.

The Pacific States Telephone Company, which operated the toll line between San Francisco and Portland, wanted more revenue and this meant expanding the service with more subscribers to telephone service. A manager arrived to talk with the gentleman in

Medford, who kept the switchboard in the rear of his store, about getting more business. It will be noted that Jacksonville was the county seat but, according to that 1899 telephone directory, there were no telephones in the Court House.

The Rogue River Valley Railroad had no telephones in it's headquarters depot in Jacksonville, none at its way-station at Perrydale Avenue and none in its terminal in Medford.

Southern Pacific had its own telephone system that was used only for railroad business. The Medford depot had no switching equipment, as well as no permission, to jump calls between the Pacific States Telephone Company lines and its own lines.*

It is also plausible, but unlikely because of the particular telephone numbers assigned in Jacksonville, that there was only one line (circuit) between the two towns and all the subscribers in Jacksonville were on a "party line." If this was true, this meant that only one of the four subscribers in Jacksonville could talk with Medford at a time. If the town was served only by a single line, the telephone numbers would more likely have been a combination of long and short rings, depending on who was being called, instead of specific numbers.

When the telephone company representative talked with the switchboard manager-operator in Medford about getting more business, the local manager curtly told the fellow from San Francisco that the first priority for business increase was to get rid of the toll costs between Medford and Jacksonville. This aggressively made suggestion was accepted and almost immediately there were many applications for more telephone installations in Jacksonville.

In 1982, Pacific Northwest Bell Telephone Company reported 1,933 telephone numbers assigned in the Jacksonville 899 prefix area. In November 1993, U. S. West reported there were a total 2,762 numbers operating. □

---

*Telephone lines were strung on poles alongside the railroads, whether the lines were privately owned by the railroad or owned and serviced by a telephone company. Wires did not follow highways because in bad weather, when line repairs seemed most often needed, access to the lines was always available on the railroad but not so along muddy roads. SP's private line had dozens of call boxes at key points along the track In each box was a hand-cranked magneto telephone. The railroad between Medford and Jacksonville, being short, did not require a private railroad-operated telephone line. —Ed.

12.

The Schools; A Lively Part of the Town

Whenever people gather into a new town with children, it isn't long before steps are taken to start a school. We have seen that Emma Royal, whose father was an early Methodist minister, conducted school in the winter of 1853. Her effort was well received so she was hired the following year by the newly formed Public School District. The first terms were necessarily short ones. In April 1855, the school directors picked a site for a building on North Oregon Street but it took nearly two years of tax levies ($550 each) to build a frame schoolhouse and pay the teacher. The second Rogue Indian War (1855-56), coupled with other community interests, resulted in interrupted school schedules. There was no compulsory education at this time so attendance could not be enforced. Teachers needed to have other income-earning capacity, and frequently let their contracts drop if a better job came along.

Jacksonville was a staunch pro-slavery stronghold and many of its substantial citizens would hear of no compromise. Without compulsory school attendance and some reported pressures to teach a pro-slavery platform, a proper school environment was to be delayed several years. In fact, by 1860, any semblance of a "working" school system seems to have completely disappeared. The town's population was growing and schools were sought. It was during the Civil War that Fr. Blanchet. decided he would promote the establishment of a school that would admit young ladies to a general curriculum with a Roman Catholic flavor. The public school was not functioning thus, say some, Fr. Blanchet's idea was well received. As we have seen, St. Mary's Academy opened its doors.

Jacksonville's first brick school (top) was built in 1903 but
lasted only two ready before burning. It was replaced
immediately (1908) with building that still stands. Lower
picture made in 1918. For the building today see page 102.

There is little doubt that the success of the Catholic school brought pressure to bear on the long inactive public school board. Parents of the Protestant persuasion sought schooling for their children but most refused to participate with the Catholics. The trustees met and decided it was time to start anew with a new school building. As might be expected, opposition to school expansion was great from citizens whose own education was deficient, but who, through good fortune, had taxable property. In time, well-wishers won, property was acquired then a building erected. Regrettably, there were to be many unsettled years for education in Jacksonville as partisan politics crept into almost every issue.

A hill on the northeast edge of town, Bigham's Knoll and some seven acres adjoining, was purchased in 1868. The price, $600, was raised, with Beekman's help, to construct a two-story frame building. A Jacksonville builder and cabinet maker was awarded the construction contract. Cost over-runs are not of recent invention for an additional $1,000 was needed to complete the work.

When the building was finished, most of the town turned out to look at their new school. The Board decided that a school year would run six months. Two teachers were hired to serve 79 boys and 46 girls.

But how does a school marm notify the town that classes are about to begin without a bell? "Old Beek," as the town's then only banker was called (but never to his face), raised the cost of a bell by sponsoring a formal dance and minstrel show in the ballroom of the U. S. Hotel.

Jacksonville's school district experienced several tragedies with its buildings. When the new school burned to the ground just a few years after being opened, the patrons stood together and built a larger one. The 125 students of three years earlier would grow, as it was believed there were close to 350 children of school age in the area. Of course St. Mary's would siphon off some, but as there was no compulsory education in Oregon until 1889, some parents didn't send their children to any schools. The Board decided to build a four room school to be staffed by four teachers. While a county school office did exist and taxes were levied, collecting the taxes was another matter. Regrettably, few Jacksonville teachers lasted more than three years and neither did the principals.

> At one time a School Board ruled that teachers who drank liquor would be dismissed forthwith.

During the smallpox epidemic of 1869, the school, and all other public buildings, closed its doors.

Teachers who enforced discipline sooner or later had some parents to contend with. Tales got home about happenings at school but seldom did a parent hear both sides of an issue. Regrettably, then as now, parents who complained of their child being disciplined at school were all too frequently the parents who did not discipline their children at home. Very often the good kids were kept in along with the bad kids. This caused certain parents to stomp up to the school as their child had to suffer because of the rowdiness and trouble-making of others. But how was a teacher to handle it? In the 1872-73 year there were 85 students with only a husband/wife team as educators. These two were also disciplinarians, tenders of the school yard, ringers of the bell, fight breaker uppers, as well as writers and editors of reports for the School Board. Then as now, there was always a group of people who were against schools, said so vocally, and voted against budgets.

Most pre-teen boys, attending school near the turn of the century, felt uncomfortable and out of place when ordered to sit still at a desk in a room with girls. Instead of studying, these fellows would much rather be, among other pranks, catching toads and taunting girls with them. These were days before school counselor-psychologists, thus teachers generally ruled the unruly with force. Any kid who was out of order was marched off to the principal's office – once schools got principal – often dragged there by an ear! Nearly all of these boys had their knuckles banged with a ruler many times and the really unruly could be bent over a principal's lap and whipped.

It was not uncommon for teachers, many of whom must surely have earned their high blood pressure trying to "teach" pre-teen boys, to leave the room then quietly enter by the back door specifically to catch the room's clown in a prank, grab him, then shake him until his teeth rattled or until teacher was out of breath, then slam the kid down in his seat.

No wonder Vance "Pinto" Colvig and his chums cheered when the school burned in 1903, for this meant no more classes at least for awhile. Was the town, and later the country, ready for this boy who could turn the school and the town inside out with his irreverence and shenanigans Here was a boy with no feeling for conservative traditions. (See chapter 13.)

The ashes were barely cool from the school fire when work started on the new building. This one, of brick, would go up in record time.

Any of many miscellaneous troubles had bothered teachers and kids alike, especially the girls. Wandering cows, sometimes prodded into the building by Tom Sawyer-type boys and left there over weekends with dire results on the floor, had to be fenced out. The School Board ordered a picket fence around the grounds with a narrow gate at the base of the hill. But there seemed no way to keep the gate on its hangers come Halloween!

In the yard, girls were assigned to one side and boys on the other. No one dared cross the imaginary line even to chase a ball, for there was a teacher-monitor always there during recess with a handbell. Any boy who ventured into the girls' side brought forth a vigorous shaking of that bell and the possibility of a whack from the principal.

At first, drinking water was hauled to the school each morning in a tank-wagon which was parked near the front door. After unhitching from the wagon, the driver walked the horse back into town. Early in a recess, boys would frequently pull the plug causing a rapid evacuation of the tank. This caused:

1) a muddy puddle right near the front door
2) girls couldn't get back into the building without soiling their shoes
3) teachers became very angry
4) of course no one would squeal as to who did it.

Eventually the Board got tired of this continuing prank so they dug a well on which they placed a hand pump and a bucket.

At recess, girls jumped rope, played drop the handkerchief, giggled while playing tag.

The boys liked sliding in the mud from the draining water tank.

Boys played marbles which teachers confiscated at every opportunity.

Boys spun hardwood tops which teachers confiscated at every opportunity.

Boys played "king in the tree." The first boy up the tree at recess was "king." The object of the other boys was to haul him down, cracked head or not.

A new sport, roller skating, was sweeping the country. When the basement was finished in concrete, the girls were allowed to skate there during recess. Research does not indicate if the boys had skates (it is presumed they probably had skates before the girls) but if they did, where they skated is elusive.

Of course these school buildings did not have inside plumbing. There were two privies near the fence. There was one for girls on their side of their yard. The School Board put the boys' privy on the opposite side of their yard away from the girls. These privies were well bolted down as the Board was well-on to the boys' tricks of upsetting them especially on Halloween night. Each was a three-holer. These toilets were pretty crude by today's standards for a "pit" or vault" field toilet. These were just holes dug into the ground. They were never cleaned, always stunk, and were noted for flies, yellow-jackets and spiders. Of earth-shattering magnitude one day was the discovery, in the girls' privy, of a hornet's nest under the seat.

In the spring, it was not uncommon for the girls to dash for the privy at recess only to find the door missing! (During an interview for this book, the authors learned of a one-time-only escapade where, over a weekend, some boys completely filled the girls' privy with dirt.)

Mornings, as the 9 o'clock bell clanged, everyone dashed for his exact place in line before the main door. Once in place and all was deathly quiet, the two lines, one of boys, one of girls, marched to the tapping of a hand bell up steps into rooms where each pupil stood in a brace beside his or her desk. At a signal, each room recited the Pledge to the flag. Then the teacher ordered all into their seats.

It was the very same every morning except once. On this day, classes were just being called to order when a boy shot to his feet and pointed to a flame in the new brick building. Children were hustled outdoors as smoke thickened and the volunteer fire department was summoned by one who ran all the way to the station and jerked on the bell rope. Although the firemen responded, nothing could be done to save the building. So great were the flames, they were reported seen as far as Eagle Point.

The brick school had been the pride of the community. Its loss was great as the insurance was for only $10,000. To replace the structure would be twice that much at least.

When school opened in fall 1906, classes were scattered all over town. The Presbyterian Church basement was used as was the town hall, the newspaper office and the second floor of the brewery. It was not until late January 1908 that the new building was ready.

Newspaper accounts claimed the brand new building was one of the handsomest and best appointed in the state. The building was nearly 100 feet long with a 56 foot frontage. Advertised as "absolutely fireproof," it was heated by a steam boiler. Classrooms were 32 x 25 feet and illuminated by electric lights –a single bulb in the center of each room's ceiling. There was a library and special "teachers' room." For use in bad weather, the 3,600 square-foot basement was designed as a play room. The general assembly room had a stage fitted with footlights. As the original bell was lost in the fire, a new 500-pound bell was ordered. On Fridays, the school band played a concert from the cupola. Probably the most appreciated feature was "inside" plumbing!

The first World War brought profound changes to Jacksonville. There were many of German decent who had been residents for years. The town newspaper, the *Post,* was anti-war. There was no industry in town so many men, who were not drafted, left to work elsewhere. Of the departing men, some were teachers. With the teacher shortage some classes were combined. But probably the most severe impact on the schools was bickering within the School Board. Principals and teachers became "tools" of some Board members with some teachers being fired in plays for power.

The high school could not open one year because of a shortage of teachers from this in-fighting. Compulsory education was now in effect so the School Board was left with no choice but to make a deal with Medford on a tuition basis. An inter-city jitney was hired to carry Jacksonville's students to Medford's high school.

* * *

Time was marching by with little impact on Jacksonville. A notable occurrence however, was the building of the first "gas" station in 1914. The newspaper wrote that having a drive-in station would lessen the fire hazard as cans of gasoline, filled in the back rooms of stores with a hand pump fitted to a barrel, would be discontinued.

One of the frustrations of the town was to see its youth leave as there were few employment opportunities in the home town. Teenagers began to see "the other side" when they were whisked to Medford for high school. Medford had a real train which brought interesting people to town. There was a "movie house" which was officially "off limits" to the commuting students, but they read the advertisements.

In the beginning, Jacksonville's school was pure basic academics. If there were any "sports," it was of the after school variety. In the early 1920's, under pressure, the District rented the

Jacksonville's antique school building, renovated, shown in 1982, presently owned by Cascade Christian High School

upstairs ballroom at the U. S. Hotel for a basketball court. The school got its own gym in 1924. Following the opening of the gymnasium, organized sports became a part of the curriculum.

Spankings for boys' infractions gave way to manual labor. The Principal supervised boys equipped with picks and shovels to excavate an area that would eventually become a basement next to the gym.

In one era, with many vacant houses, the county moved the poor to Jacksonville as a mean of housing them cheaply. Traditionally, the poor do not vote favorably for school budgets so Jacksonville's school elections were in jeopardy. With funds short, the building maintenance was cut to a minimum which resulted in a need for almost constant repairs.

Real estate values declined and so did taxes. At one point, teachers were paid with warrants as the District had run out of money.

The Superintendent surveyed the District patrons and reported to the School Board that the majority favored consolidation with Medford. Thus, the election of 1959 brought about termination of classes above the 6th grade. As we saw, the town had earlier lost its high school. Now it lost its juniors. As the old building further deteriorated, the cupola was removed and later the second floor was closed to occupancy.

Many old timers in town did not favor the consolidation with the Medford District and vented their frustration with "no" votes at annual levy balloting. (Some still do.)

Nevertheless, the Medford School District No. 549C decided the 1908 building had served long enough and must be replaced. In spring 1982, work started, next door, on a new elementary building which saw its first classes in 1983.

The old brick edifice on Bingham's Knoll was leased to various private schools for a number of years and then sold. At the present writing, the building is owned by Cascade Christian High School, an accredited interdenominational parent-owned institution of grades 9-12. This school opened its 1993-94 school year in the Jacksonville school building with 143 students. □

Vance "Pinto," "Bozo-the-Clown" Colvig in the front row (2nd from right) about 1904 in the first brick school. Of this picture, Colvig declared years later, "At the time photo was taken I was either half-asleep, wasn't interested, or possibly drawing pictures in one of my books. The art work on the blackboard is mine but definitely *not* the arithmetic, I assure you." Colvig (right) in typical clown outfit.

13.
"Pinto"

As mentioned earlier, the school had its run of clowns especially in spring when boys' thoughts wandered easily from text books. It would take Jacksonville quite a number of years to realize that one of the nation's best known clowns had grown up in its midst.

Vance DeBar Colvig was born in Jacksonville in 1892. He was the cut-up of the town and earned the name "Pinto-the village clown" at the age of 7, because of his crop of freckles and goony antics. (The family home still stands at Fir and S. Oregon Streets.) His father, Judge Colvig, took him to Portland to the Lewis & Clark Exposition in 1905, but "Pinto" didn't get any farther than a side show on the Midway. He saw a guy beating a drum to get attention for his show, so he went up to him and ventured, "I can play a squeaky Clarinet!" Although the man told him to come back on the morrow, the boy dashed back to the hotel, got his E-flat Clarinet then raced back to the stand. He was put to work right then. The following day when he arrived, the man put "clown white" on his face, gave him a hat and dressed him in oversize clothing. He became "Bozo-the-Clown" that day and used that title for the rest of his life.

Colvig later wrote, "I guess I was just meant to be a clown." As he grew up, he learned to draw cartoons and was quite expert by the time he reached 6th grade. "Pinto" wrote many years later, "A cartoonist is just a clown with a pencil."

In school, he would squirm through winter sessions but come spring he'd hit the road. He went across country riding the rails and had many a meal with hobos along the tracks. Colvig loved the circus and ran off to join the A. G. Barnes Circus.

This post card is labeled "Main Street" however view is looking east on California Street from Oregon Street. Masonic Lodge Building on right.

Pinto was always ready to put on a show with his squeaky clarinet and clown outfit. He entered Oregon Agricultural college (now Oregon State University) and played E-flat Clarinet in the Cadet Band. His objective? He didn't know if he wanted to become a professional clown, a musician, a writer, or what. He stayed at the college only three years. Later, he took a position in Nevada on a newspaper as a political cartoonist, then he moved to the San Francisco *Bulletin*. Finally in 1922, he and his wife moved to Hollywood where he became a comedian and writer.

"Pinto" did some work for Walt Disney in 1930 then he held a contract with Disney Studio in the mid-'30's. During that period, he worked on *Snow White and the Seven Dwarfs* as the voices of "Grumpy" and "Sleepy." In the Mickey Mouse series, he was "Pluto's" voice and that of "Goofy." In the animated movie, *The Three Little Pigs*, his voice was heard as the "Practical Pig." His musicianship came in handy and his ability to write lyrics brought him fame and great royalties with the words to the hit tune, "Who's Afraid of the Big Bad Wolf?"

During the height of his "Bozo-the-Clown" popularity, one could buy "Bozo" coloring books, record albums, dolls and other toys.

On the radio, he did sound effects for Jack Benny's famous Maxwell automobile, which never ran smoothly, but "huffed, snorted, wheezed" every time "Mr. Benny" drove it.

"Pinto" Colvig never forgot his home town, Jacksonville, although his work took him elsewhere. The clipping file in the library of the Southern Oregon Historical Society reveals he visited town numerous times in later years. During a 1963 visit, he was a Marshall in the summer parade.

A theatrical agent once listed him as good in "offbeat characters, clowns, creeps," and mentioned that Colvig had hosted three award-winning children's' series, and acknowledged that he was a professional musician: "E-flat Clarinet." *

But kid's records in the old 78 rpm don't last forever. While working on this book, the authors asked listeners to a Medford radio station for donations of old "Bozo-the-Clown" books and records for the Children's Department of the Jackson County Library. There was no response.

Vance DeBar "Pinto," "Bozo-the-Clown" Colvig died at age 75 in 1967. Mementos of his life's clowning can be viewed and appreciated in the Jacksonville Museum. □

---

* The E-flat clarinet is shorter in length than the common B-flat clarinet and was popular in the proud days of brass bands. It was very useful in band arrangements of classic orchestral works where it played high parts usually delegated to violins. This unique instrument plays higher notes than its B-flat sister and could be indeed "squeaky," especially when in the hands of a professional musician-clown as "Pinto" Colvig. Today's composers and arrangers delegate much of the music once the domain of E-flat clarinets to flutes therefore the demise of E-flat clarinets. In addition to this variety, there are alto, bass and contra-bass clarinets. Some of these can be seen in the Southern Oregon Symphonic Band, John E. Drysdale, Conductor.

14.
The Last Trial

Jacksonville had its share of "police actions" starting with the murder of a gold miner in the very early days. Later, a very popular sheriff was killed in a shoot-out with a young desperado at the edge of town. There were numerous clashes with the Ku Klux Klan. And there were little things as when the town cop had to chase boys off the railroad track when they were caught greasing the rails. In addition, there were the usual cases which fill a court docket day in and day out.

But the most notorious crime of its day to be committed in Jackson County occurred in 1923 when the DeAutremont brothers held up a Southern Pacific train in a tunnel high in the Siskiyou Mountains. The brothers dynamited the mail car seeking money which they believed was on board. They didn't get a dime! But they killed the Railway Mail Clerk – a federal offense – and the trainmen. Although the area around the tunnel (No. 13), where the deed occurred, and the tracks were thoroughly searched, as was the nearby forest, there was no trace of the fugitives. It would be several years before the brothers were captured. One had joined the U. S. Army and was in the Philippine Islands. He was caught because a fellow soldier recognized his picture on one of the 2,583,000 "WANTED" posters. It was announced that the trial would be in the Jackson County Courthouse. The town was immediately in the nation's headlines as the trial got under way in 1927. Newspaper reporters and newsreel cameramen flocked to the Court House. The Medford *Mail Tribune*, with its offices just 6-miles away, had a field day with first-hand reports and prompt press releases for the wire service. Detective story writers swelled the town for here were all the makings for sensational writing for the 10¢ pulp magazines.

When the Court House was built it was the largest building in the county. View here is in winter (leaves not on trees) and before streets were paved.

The trial was heated as testimony and arguments went back and forth, but in the end the DeAutremont brothers – all three as the other two had been apprehended in Ohio, again as a result of the posters –were escorted to the State Penitentiary at Salem for life. *

One of the brothers was paroled in 1950, but died shortly thereafter. Another was paroled in 1972 but died in 1983. The third had been transferred to the State Hospital because of mental breakdown and died in a Nursing Home in 1984. These were the days of long incarceration for multiple murders.

The trial of the DeAutremonts was the last major event to stage in the Court House. Medford had been agitating to become the county seat for several years and a hot campaign had been waged in 1927. Following an election, the Medford people, who were far in the majority, found themselves winners by a landslide.

---

* For many original pictures and details of the holdup, see the book: *Oregon's Great Train Holdup, Bandits Murder 4 – Didn't Get A Dime*! In autumn 1993, on the 70th anniversary of the holdup, Portland television station KPTV presented a documentary based on this book. See bibliography.

Judge's desk and witness chair in Jacksonville Museum (x-Court House) the way it appeared during the DeAutremont trial in 1927.

Quaint little "J'ville" did not have enough people to swing the vote. The fine Court House in Jacksonville was vacated when the County built a new one in Medford. Eventually, the building became the permanent home of the Jacksonville Museum of the Southern Oregon Historical Society.

With the loss of the county seat, Jacksonville lost even more businesses, especially lawyers because lawyers traditionally like to have their offices in the shadow of the courts. (They don't have to walk so far in rainy weather.)

Medford developed rapidly. It became Southern Oregon's leading bruise on the landscape and greatest polluter of the once clean air.

*   *   *

With the financial crash of 1929, many wondered how much of Jacksonville's economy would sink? There was no commerce, no factories to close. The railroad had ceased and even most of the track was gone. People were without jobs everywhere and "For Rent" and "For Sale" signs appeared all over the little town. The town was just plain tired out. It just seemed to want to rest after all the hassles and failures to retain its once greatness. Jacksonville just went to sleep and would remain in a state of hibernation for the next four decades. ☐

111

There were dozens of mine shafts sunk in back yards and in vacant lots where some men took out enough gold to buy groceries. Other struck it fairly rich. Others reaped nothing for their hard labor. Here is A. C. VanGalder's backyard operation on C Street just east of Oregon Street, where he and partner did well. (Lower) The late Wesley Hartman, former City Mine Inspector, points to area for Bert Webber, research photojournalist, where sidewalk and curb sank years later due to tunnel dug earlier. Area is on south side of California Street just west of 4th Street. See pictures of 4th Street cave-in on page 118-119.

15.
Where the Streets Are Lined With Gold

The depression had hit hard and it would not be until the early 1940's before there was any snapping back. In the mean time, those who had homes in town began to think of the historic past. The town had been founded because of a gold strike. Maybe there was still some around. People put their possibility thinking to work realizing the town might be sitting on gold.

Gold?

GOLD !

With men out of work and with nothing else to do, some tried digging for gold in their back yards.

While some old timers had a little mining experience, most of the folks did not. Holes were dug anyway and the dirt was carefully washed. Sharp eyes scrutinized the pan looking for sparkles of gold dust. If none, or little was found, holes went deeper, many becoming shafts straight to bed rock maybe twenty or more feet down. Some of these shafts were four to six feet wide while others were no more than man-hole size. As the dirt was hoisted out, it was washed with water hauled from the kitchen sink. A few made enough money to keep their families off the relief rolls.

A number became adventurous. Once down their shafts, they started to tunnel under the rest of the yard then under their houses. There was little risk of cave ins as the hardpan above the tunnels would support a lot of weight. Some shafts and tunnels were lined with timbers by the more progressive men, and on a few operations, sheds were constructed over the shaft to ward off the rain.

But the back-yard mining didn't necessarily stop at property lines. A. C. Van Galder went down through his back yard near a tree and then tunneled almost to the old railroad station. His tunnel was reported to have been about four feet high and twelve feet wide.

> During the winter of 1980, a pickup truck's front end crashed through the city street near the telephone pole immediately west of the old train depot. Many believe this was one of Van Galder's tunnels.

But Van Galder didn't stop with one hole. He dug another in his yard but it was "dry." No gold there. Earlier, a fellow had dug at the corner of the property and this was also dry. They filled the hole with old rock and bricks then planted a redwood tree in the middle. Today one can see the tree still nicely growing on the east side of North Oregon Street just north of "C" Street.

Partnerships for back yard mining were common because to make progress, it took two or more men. One partnership sank a shaft in a yard then tunneled under California Street at 4th Street. The digging continued under the building for another forty feet. A fellow who had been a City Mining Inspector, (the late) Wes Hartman, told the authors when he notified the partners of his pending inspection, they found reason to delay him while they filled in the entrances to lateral tunnels they thought he didn't know about.

Then there was the mine under California Street near 5th, with "headquarters" where, at this writing, there is a store in a former service station. In the center of town there is, on the northeast corner, another former service station (at 4th Street). This whole lot was once a storage yard for mining equipment and was the site of another major mine shaft. Van Galder and Jack Green dug up an estimated $25,000 in gold there. It has been rumored through the years that Jacksonville passed a City Ordinance prohibiting mining in the City Limits, however no trace of such an Ordinance can be found today, according to personnel in the City's offices. Anyway, who'd want to stop a little friendly back yard digging?

In the 1852 gold rush, Chinese laborers were plentiful, and there was a "Chinatown" area in Jacksonville. In the 1930's, some tunnelers rumored they had hit old Chinese tunnels but found no gold. Small wonder for if these were indeed Chinese tunnels, the

114

Orientals were very thorough in their very quiet mining operations and never knowingly left any of the precious metal behind them.

Just east of the Presbyterian Church was another mining operation which was the subject of complaints. A housewife pleaded to the town Marshall that she heard strange noises, "scratchings" and sometimes "grunts" under her house in the middle of the night. These noises turned out to be miners Bill Kennedy and Henry Dimmer. When their tunnel reached the area near the east wall of the church, they quit.

One father-and-son team reported years later that between $20,000 and $30,000 in gold was taken from their backyard and understreet ventures in about seven years.

Several enterprising fellows set up sluice boxes on Daisy Creek in the city. One was located on "C" Street where the creek passes under the street near 7th. Another was located on Daisy Creek below the school near 8th and "E" Streets.

In 1933, under a New Deal project, Medford's school Superintendent was asked to provide three-day courses in effective gold mining for the benefit of the people who wanted to try their luck and hopefully stay off the county's scanty relief list.

Two miners were contracted to teach the classes. Pupils spent two days were in the classroom and the third day was a field exercise. The course was short and precise because most of the men had only limited classroom experience and even on this potential money-making subject, would become bored easily with too much school. The third day was a field trip that included these topics:

> How to care for the gold pan
> How to pan for gold
> How to trace and locate placer gold
> How to trace and locate quartz gold
> How to build and operate a sluice box
> How to build and operate a rocker
> How to file a valid location of a claim

A third "teacher" was hired as "field man." He traveled the area and assisted miners as he found them. One of his tasks was to help miners with negotiating royalty agreements with property owners. Most of Jacksonville's back yard miners were operating on their own property, so those who attended the classes were

115

PARTNERSHIP AGREEMENT

THIS AGREEMENT made this twenty-sixth day of July, nineteen hundred and thirty five, between Joseph E. McIntyre, Leonard Osborn, Frank Taylor, and George Campbell all of the City of Jacksonville, State of Oregon.

WITNESSETH, as follows

I. That the said parties abovenamed agree to become partners in mining operations of J.S. Sawyer and Joseph E. McIntyre in Jacksonville, Oregon.

2. This agreement shall be effective for ninety days from the above date.

3. The said parties above named agree to pay to J. S. Sawyer and Joseph M. McIntyre 20% of all gold as royalty.

4. The said parties, Joseph E. McIntyre, Leonard Osborn, Frank Taylor and George Camp agree to share equally the remaining 80% of all gold taken from this mine, after the operating expenses have been deducted from the same.

5. The said parties agree to cease operations should J.S. Sawyer and Joseph E. McIntyre desire to sell the property.

6. The said parties agree to hold J.S. Sawyer and Joseph E. McIntyre harmless from any and all claims, demands, and suits for damages or injuries received in said mining operations.

7. The parties agree to cease operations is J.S. Sawyer objects, or any controversy arrises from mining under the street.

8. The said parties agree not to mine within under the residence of J.E. McIntyre or anistngth closer to said residence than I2 feet surface distance.

9. The said parties agso agree that no equipment shall be purchased unless all the said parties agree to the purchase.

Frank Taylor

Leonard Osborn

Geo Campbell

C+8th St.

basically new-comers to the art of gold mining who panned for gold elsewhere.

While the depression lasted, many of the unemployed spent most of their time working in their backyard mines. The gold dust extracted was generally sent to the United States Mint in San Francisco. As it wasn't practical for miners to take their gold there in person, they sold at discount to a handler. In Jacksonville, one middleman was the Godward Mercantile Company, a general store. (If one wanted to reach the store in 1938 by phone, just ask "Central" for No. 74.)

With the advent of the Second World War, many of the back yard shafts were filled in, but it appears nobody bothered to stuff the tunnels. Years later, a lady drove her car into the carport of her home when suddenly the front wheels sank and the car rested on the frame.

When a fireman was driving one of the city's fire trucks on a routine inspection mission and stopped at the corner of 5th and "C" Streets for the stop sign, the street under one of the rear wheels suddenly collapsed. A Van Galder tunnel?

The sidewalk and curb on the south side of California Street sank several inches without notice. This is just west of 4th. It was here that a tunnel ran under the street from a shaft on a lot on the northwest corner.

Probably the last recognized mining occurred in 1957 when city workers were digging for footing sites for the new Jackson Creek Emil Britt Bridge on N. Oregon Street. The city agreed to dump the mud into personal pickup trucks if persons interested would be at the site when the shovel was working. Several loads went into the pickups to be dumped in backyards where the dirt could be washed for gold at leisure. There is no doubt that gold was found because this was immediately downstream from where

> Following World War-II, Bill Dobbyn and Fred Christean formed a partnership. With a drag line dredge operating in Jackson Creek just west of Oregon Street, they brought in over $1,000 per week on some weeks. Report on bullion shipment for April 22, 1946, gave the partners $1,217.48 to split after expenses.

117

Patrons in Jubilee Club Restaurant on October 14, 1982 saw pavement "dip" under passing car then cave in when a heavy truck rolled over the same area a few minutes later. By another hour, the street collapsed, as shown, into an old gold mine cavern which had been excavated from a shaft on northwest corner of 4th and California Streets in the 1930's.

Larry Smith, 6th Grade teacher at Jacksonville School, created a field trip because of the cave-in and brought his class to look at it. While there, an old-timer demonstrated panning for gold by washing samples of earth found in the bottom of the cavern. No gold was found.

(Left page) Researcher Bert Webber (lower) climbed down into "mine" through the street cave-in as Steve DeKorte, (this page) of Jacksonville Public Works Department, stood "guard." Webber, a 6-footer, is standing on caved-in earth about 10 feet above floor of cavern which was on bedrock. There is about 3 feet distance between top of Webber's head and street level. Webber took off his hard hat for the glory of the picture! The Attorney for the City of Jacksonville allowed Webber to enter the cavern only after extracting a liability release.

Dobbyn's dredge had been stopped by an earlier bridge.

In 1932, the Chamber of Commerce developed a scheme to bring people and money to town. Why not hold a "Gold Rush Jubilee"? People had been deeply hurt by the depression and needed to release tensions by having a rip-roaring, old-time celebration. The event was apparently well handled and made some money. The next year plans were refined and an even grander affair was staged. To gain a degree of mirth, the

Jacksonville *Miner* insisted that the streets would be thoroughly swept to remove excess gold nuggets and "rotten quartz" left by miners as they strolled through town. The mayor admonished:

> If the dogs in town would do their digging on the flats or in the back yards instead of in the city streets ... there wouldn't be all this gold lying around for people to stumble over. Yesterday the Marshall reported that Emil Britt's Cocker Spaniel got out of the yard and started to bury a bone in front of Charlie Chitwood's place and rolled a big hunk of gold down the hill as big as your hat. Roy Smith came driving along and nearly busted a wheel on it. Such business has to stop or people will be afraid to come to the celebration.

Why the annual jubilee didn't continue in the next few years is unknown, unless the power behind the event was someone who tired of having all the responsibility.

Nearly twenty years later, boosters in Jacksonville wanted to bring back the jubilee, so in 1950 there was a big push to do this. It was an eventful year, as the old Court House had been officially recognized as the new and permanent home of the Southern Oregon Historical Society's Museum. The museum had occupied the building earlier, but now it was to be official. A dedication was part of the program.

The town was beginning to move ahead again. The following year the celebration was staged again. It attracted wide attention when the National Broadcasting Company moved in with a production team to make a 30-minute feature radio program based on local history. But it looked as if Jacksonville had again shot its wad for subsequent years saw a falling off of enthusiasm for the annual event. Its last year was 1956.

A contributing factor to the failure of a jubilee was undoubtedly that the celebration lacked a theme. As Oregon celebrated its Centennial in 1959, the event was revived, but lack of enthusiasm was obvious and the " celebration" did not leave the home folks feeling the results were worth the effort.

In recent years, the Jacksonville Volunteer Fire Department has sponsored a "Pioneer Days" in June. The date is permanent, always on Saturday, the day before Father's Day. This seems appropriate as the down town district is truly a scene from the past and is recognized as a National Historic Landmark. At last the celebration has a theme. □

16.
Later Developments...

In the late 1930's, war threats were heard throughout America. Men were being called to work in war related industry after years of unemployment and some, in the Oregon National Guard, were called to active duty.

Jacksonville was again seeing its men leaving town. But suddenly, high wage work appeared in the country as the Army announced plans to build a camp in an area typical of Army camp locations – in the middle of the Agate Desert. This was about 12 miles northeast, "as the crow flies," from Jacksonville. The desert was nearly as flat as a pool table, grew desert-like flora, and was inhabited by field mice, jack rabbits and some rattlesnakes. Camp White became its name. When ready, this army post trained the 91st Division for overseas fighting. Blue prints called for a central power and heating plant which required lots of ditch digging for the "conduit" that would carry the pipes and wires. Jacksonville, as well as other communities in the valley, had men looking for work many of whom jumped at this opportunity. The camp would include a huge Army hospital as well as the recruit training area. There would be a gunnery range. Not only would this project hire a lot of people, it also meant that vacant houses in Jacksonville would be filled with workers imported from other areas, as well as for Army Officers because some would bring families. And it all happened.

A portion of the camp became a P.O.W. center for German prisoners, some of whom, after the war, came back to make the Rogue Valley their permanent homes.

Eventually, Camp White became White City, Oregon, and in 1980 gained its own postal ZIP code – 97503. Industry had leased much space in what was named Medford Industrial Park. Thou-

121

sands of persons built homes, or hauled in mobile units on the fringes of the arid Agate Desert. The former Army hospital was converted to become the major Veterans Administration Domiciliary in the United States.

*   *   *

Various motion picture producers over the years have visited Jacksonville, and the surrounding hills, then came back to make films. One of the most exciting (filmed in the heart of the historic district) was *The Great Northfield Minnesota Raid* in late 1970. The movie people arranged a deal with the city to work over some of the historic buildings that didn't have an "historic-enough" look. They covered the paved street with dirt and placed wooden sidewalks over concrete to add authenticity. Hundreds of folks were hired as "extras" to appear in the picture. It was a great time of re-living the past and everyone loved it, especially when the movie was released and many flocked to a theater to see themselves on the screen.

When it was all over, some lamented the ripping up of the temporary" wooden sidewalks.

*   *   *

When a small town, whose buildings are primarily frame, had a fire, it was generally a major conflagration. The great fire of 1873 roared through much of the town and took out Louis Horn's United States Hotel. As we have seen, The present United States Hotel was built shortly thereafter.

Then there were what came to be called "merchant" fires where a brick store building would be gutted – all the insured stock destroyed. Volunteer firemen are great guys and do their best but in days when mere hose carts and bucket brigades were the only equipment and methods, little headway was possible on a big fire. In an effort to stop town-destroying fires, the town council passed an ordinance requiring all new construction in the business blocks to be of stone or brick. Even so, over the years there were major fires that destroyed business buildings, and some home fires forced occupants into the night saving only what was on their backs.

122

Jacksonville's fire fighters used a hand pumper in the early days but retired it when hydrants were installed on the city streets in 1912. Fully motorized "fire trucks" would not appear for quite some years nevertheless, the volunteers always met at regular intervals for training sessions and practices right from the first. Many of the training classes were, and are to the present day, discussions of techniques for fighting a fire in every building in town. Today the firemen are still volunteers and some are merchants and businessmen whose shops are close to the Fire House. The Department is part of the mutual assistance plan where it gives help to other localities if called upon, and in turn can call for help from other departments. ☐

One of the few Indians in town. He has to come in at night because he's made of wood.

Jacksonville Museum is located in former Courthouse

17.
Its History Is Its Industry

Many persons wanted to keep Jacksonville a small town with close ties to a great historic past. Others wanted to open the area for general residential construction as well as for condominiums plus a huge shopping mall to be surrounded by an asphalt jungle. There were, and still are, quite a number who don't care what happens. But for the vigilance of a few, the old town might have been leveled long ago.

With very few exceptions in American history, towns developed alongside some kind of a thoroughfare. The first trail through what was to become Jacksonville, became known as the main street along which businesses sprang up. As the town grew, more "streets" were added. A surveyor platted the town in the late summer of 1852 and the main thoroughfare became "B" Street – later renamed California Street. This is also a State Highway 238.

This main artery carried in its day walkers, horses and riders, wagons, stage coaches, then automobiles. Also: light trucks, heavy trucks, auto freight trucks, loaded logging trucks, gasoline tankers, campers, vans, trailers, etc. Early in the 1960's, the State Highway people planned to reroute Highway 238 to bypass the town. There were several empty, rickety frame houses in the northwest part of town, not in the core historic area, whose values were pretty low. Any one of them would topple with a mere nudge of a bulldozer.

The route, as then envisioned, would take off from the present highway in the vicinity of Blackstone Alley and North 5th Street, take out those few old buildings staying south of Jackson Creek, pass west of the historic Rogue River Valley Railway Depot then rejoin the highway on California Street near the present city shops. This would keep through-traffic out of the center of the

125

historic town. It would not be a high-speed route as the city would set the allowable speeds. There were people in town who thought this might be a good plan, but others didn't like it. True, the historic core would not be touched but, so reasoning went, to tear down historic buildings on the periphery would detract from the whole.

Arguments see-sawed back and forth. The then mayor, E. O. "Curley" Graham, sought an appointment with the late Glen Jackson, head of the State Highway Department. As mayor of Jacksonville, the appointment was readily given. Graham took with him Robertson "Robbie" Collins, an expert in community preservation and a resident of Jacksonville. They talked with Jackson as well as with then Governor Mark Hatfield. The State didn't want to listen. It had already prepared the plans for the bypass. Shortly thereafter, when "Robbie" was in the east, he talked about the matter with several people including the late Senator Wayne Morse.

Much later, after he'd returned home, so "Robbie" points out, word reached him that an assignment editor for *Life Magazine* had learned something about a highway about to be built that would squash a quaint little historic village in Oregon. The editor called Glen Jackson. The editor verified that such a road construction project was indeed in the works. Of course Mr. Editor of *Life* didn't know everything about the issues but it sounded like a sensational story that *Life* might want. The editor is reported to have declared that he'd send a team and a cameraman to photograph Jackson sitting on the front of the first bulldozer taking the first bite out of the town. That killed it.

Traffic, at this writing, still plods its way through the main streets of Jacksonville: loaded logging trucks, auto-freighters, gasoline tankers, RV's, tourists, bicyclists and pedestrians. There is no relief on Sundays due to long convoys of automobiles whose occupants head for a sprawling rural church west of town.

Are there other potential bypass routes available? Yes and there is urgency, claim preservationists. The thundering of heavy trucks and the emissions from exhaust pipes is reported to be damaging to the old buildings. Serious thought is before various bodies to see that the rerouting of the highway happens and

Bronze plaque on Rock
at 3rd and California
Streets.

happens soon. What is soon? At the present time, the arguments continue.

The marvels of road building were realized in Southern Oregon when Interstate (freeway) No. 5 was designed then built more-or-less right through the middle of Bear Creek Valley and right over the top of down-town Medford. To the south, it climbs the Siskiyou Mountains with graceful curves to the border, then rejoins U.S. No. 99 which eventually became a freeway in the north end of California.

In the north, "I-5" skirted Grants Pass, climbed Mt. Sexton and other ridges, ultimately arriving in the Willamette Valley and on to Portland and Seattle.

The Rogue River Valley had, since the beginning, been all but cut off from convenient tourist travel because of the twisting, old, mountain roads. It was common to require twelve hours to drive from the valley to Portland. Southern Pacific's passenger schedule was nearly a twelve-hour ride as the track went up, down, around, about like the road. Medford had one of the first recognized airports in Oregon (1926), but passenger service by air, until the 1960's, wasn't that great either. After 1955, when S. P. stopped its passenger service, the major public transportation was by bus and the torturous snake-like highway. When the freeway opened in the mid-1960's, all this changed. Unchanging and traditional Southern Oregon, including "sleepy" Jacksonville and Medford

The Beekman house was built about 1875 and was acquired by Jackson County in 1959. The house is open in summer for guided tours.

which was quite provincial in its own unique way, suddenly had access to Portland in "jig" time. As an official of the law admonished about the new free(speed)way, "If you get to Portland in less than four hours and five minutes, you're speeding." (At 55 mph and 65 mph today it takes a little longer.)

Soon after the freeway opened, the highway people installed signs pointing toward Jacksonville announcing:

NATIONAL HISTORIC LANDMARK

Many, wondering what this was all about left the freeway, drove five miles and, *voila!* They liked what they saw. They found an historic town with original buildings fantastically alive and well.

Many Jacksonville residents seem pretty pleased with their town now that it has official recognition and protection under the preservation measures. But there are others who don't agree with all that's happened to preserve the town's center, possibly because of tax breaks which are a part of it. Jacksonville, say quite a few, is a town in which people try to live normal lives but wonder how to cope with tourists who park on lawns, block driveways, raise dust as they roar about plus the impact of huge crowds when special events are staged. Time changes things. The streets around the Britt Pavilion, a residential area, are now restricted parking, especially during performances. And the parking lot is now paved.

Nevertheless, many have restored older homes just because they think it's a good idea to protect what they own. The Booster Club provided plaques for older buildings on which the date of construction is stated.

A book, in the form of a self-guided walking tour of the Historic District is readily available in book and gift shops.*

If the scene is properly set, there will be tourists and tourists bring money. With the town full of people particularly in summer, the 25 mph speed limit is rigidly enforced. There are no parking meters, no stop-and-go signals and no drive-in fast food joints – but plenty of other eateries. It's a town to be enjoyed by walking and gawking.

The Jacksonville Museum (conducted in the former county court house) is an amazing place. At this writing there is a modest admission charge. A volunteer welcomes visitors with the request to write names and "where are you from" in the guest book. It's the way the Southern Oregon Historical Society keeps tabs on popularity of the museum.

Permanent displays include Peter Britt Photography Studio; the judge's desk used in the DeAutremont murder trial; a firearms exhibit is a superior drawing card.

> The Southern Oregon Historical Society has a major reference library in its Medford headquarters where professional and amateur historians delve into the nitty-gritty of the past.

In an adjoining building – the old county jail – is the special "Children's Museum." Kids collect here for special events, puppet shows, and where the walls are covered with pictures. The kids' section is an exciting learning environment where children "touch gently and explore a lot." (Don't rush them, dad!)

In summer there are three major events which fill the town to capacity. "Pioneer Days" celebration in June is sponsored, at this writing, by the Volunteer Fire Department. In July it's the

---

* Look for the book *Historic Jacksonville, Alive and Well; See and Enjoy Walking Tour.* by Bert and Margie Webber. See bibliography.

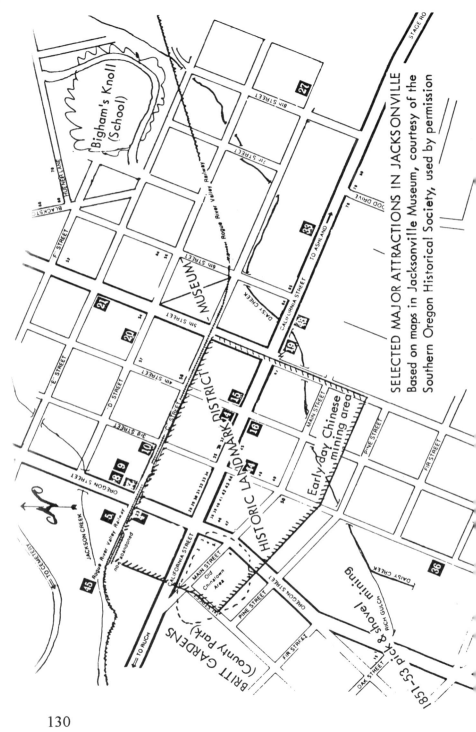

SELECTED MAJOR ATTRACTIONS IN JACKSONVILLE
Based on maps in Jacksonville Museum, courtesy of the
Southern Oregon Historical Society, used by permission

130

MAP IDENTIFICATIONS

JACKSONVILLE MINING IN 1930's
(Reversed numbers on map)

4. A follow lived in old Depot, mined behind bldg.
5. Across from Depot two men did nicely.
7. A. C. VanGalder dug pit in backyard, tunneled under "C" St. to Depot.
8. VanGalder bought house and lot just as two others gave up. Dug dry mine, planted Redwood tree - still stands.
9. VanGalder dug shaft. No gold. Dips in lawn at 250 N. Oregon St.
14. Two men dug here, tunneled under California Street then under sidewalk.
15. Corner service station and lot was major mine shaft and equipment store yard for VanGalder and Jack Green. Mined at least $ 25, 000 here.
19. Panned in creek at 5th and California.
20. Behind Methodist Church, water leaks caused tunnel collapse from which miner escaped. High production until abandoned.
21. "Blackie" Wilson hired others to assist digging under his garage. Pay dirt was excellent.
27. Joe McIntyre agreed to allow a partnership of Frank Taylor, Len Osborn and George Campbell to dig for gold on his property if they would not dig within 12-foot of his house. (See copy of contract.)
33. A tunnel went under house where lady complained of hearing noises in the night. Grunts were men taking out excellent pay dirt.
36. Lee Hardy dug several shafts, reported excellent results.
43. Four men operated the "White Owl" mine but did not tell of results.
45. Bill Dobbyn and Fred Christean ran a dragline dredge in Jackson Creek from the bridge upstream to where bedrock came to surface.

JACKSONVILLE HISTORIC SITES
(Very small numbers on map)

1. Cemetery -1860
2. Power sub-station -1905
3. Butcher shop -1854
4. Orth Bldg -1872
5 Brunner Bldg -1854
8. City Hall -1880
15. Monument: Gold Discovered -1851
23. Rogue River Valley R. R. Depot - 1891
28. Site of 1st trading tent in town - 1852
29. Bella Union Saloon -1856
30. Kennedy's Tin Shop -1861
31. Sach's Bros. Dry Goods -1861
32. Neuber's Jewelry Store (& card room) -1862
33. Sutton's Drug Store -ca1856
34. Beckman Bldg. Express & Bank - 1863
35. United States Hotel -1881
36. H. Judge Harness -ca1858
37. Ryan & Morgan Gen'l Store -1863
38. Masonic Hall -1875
39. Blacksmith Shop -1859
40. Gunsmith Shop ca -1858
41. Drum Hotel & Gen. Mdse -ca1858
42. Anderson & Glenn Gen. Mdse - 1856
43. Kubli Bldg -1884
44. Redmen's Hall -1884
45. Wade, Morgan & Co. ca1861
46. Table Rock Billiard Saloon -1859
47. McCully Bldg -1855
48. Ryan Hotel Bldg -ca1856
49. Milo Caton House -ca1902
52. B. F. Dowell House -1859
54. Methodist Church -1854
57. St. Joseph's Roman Catholic Church -1858
58. Catholic Rectory -1861
64. Armstrong House -1858
65. Presbyterian Church -1881
78. Beekman House -1876
79. Reames House -1868
80. Hattie Reames White House -1891
84. Unidentified House -ca1880

Children's Festival sponsored by the <u>Jackson County Library and the Story Telling Guild.</u> \\\\(See Chapter 18)\\In August, the Britt Music Festival commands national attention. (See Chapter 19)

Visitors like "atmosphere" and Jacksonville has it. People like to eat and "J'ville" has restaurants of many varieties. There are Expresso Bars. There are antique and new and used book shops. There are gift shops; art galleries; a drug store; the bakery turns out astounding delights; one supermarket (outside the Historic boundary); usual banks, the Post Office and the Public Library. There are new and old-fashioned fabric and sewing shops; jewelry stores, a photo studio where visitors can be costumed in 19th century clothing for a snapshot. One can look and buy stained glass in leaded frames; leather craft; and there are "saloons."

Jacksonville, the little town that lost its railroad, lost its county seat, lost its junior and senior high schools and never had an economic base, now makes its history its industry. □

Doorway to "jail" today provides access to a Fire Department store room on side of old City Hall.

20.
Kids in Peter's Front Yard

When one can get a library system, a parks department, the County Commissioners and a number of local organizations to agree to cooperate, it is truly a "Magical, Wonderful Happening."

The Children's Festival, held at Britt Gardens, a County Park in Jacksonville, is sponsored by the Jackson County Library System and the Medford Storytelling Guild. It is truly an amazing "doing" when thousands of kids get together to "see and do." The Festival has been growing a great extent every year.

It all started with the Library System's storytelling program. During the year, moms bring their children (some are toddlers), to a special corner in the library junior department once a week to listen to, or watch a story being acted out. Storytellers are usually mothers who have experience reading aloud to their own children. In time, a Storytelling Guild was formed by interested mothers, and others, who enjoy children and use the Guild as a creative outlet. The Children's Services Supervisor coordinates activities. The Guilds are usually small groups where each member is active for the good of the kids. The Guild is not a social organization.

The library furnishes quality paperback picture books rather than have mothers donate supermarket type books.

In areas away from the library, a "Story mobile" makes a regular route throughout the community offering books and stories to daycare sites where children would not normally visit the library. Children who have never been in the library are the target group. Books are loaned to the daycare.

The summer Children's Festival could be called a climax for the festival is a "show, feel, try-it-out" experience for the youngsters. It takes a lot of volunteers a long time to put it all together.

The Children's Festival includes performing arts and manual

133

The Storytelling Guild takes part in 4th-of-July parades in towns throughout Jackson County. The kids have a lot of fun.

arts. There is a puppet show. Performers stroll the park performing in impromptu settings as opportunities present themselves. There is a "Storytelling Tree" under which volunteers tell stories. Strolling musicians play a well practiced repertoire of folk music. Jugglers and magicians give instant lessons. The kids love it all. Clowns meet visitors to the park while children get in line to enter.

Children participate in all activities of the festival including an animal farm where they see and touch live animals and ask questions about them. Animals include horses, goats, rabbits, sheep, pigs, ducks, chickens, etc. Some of these might be seen in a zoo, but there is no zoo near Jacksonville so animal owners bring them to the Festival.

Volunteer mothers, members of the Storytelling Guild, are everywhere for there is much to do.

Other volunteers include gymnasts, magicians, folk singers, dancers, etc. There are square dance clubs, Community Theater players and opera singers. Radio and TV personalities serve as

Children on one of the floats during a 4-of-July parade.

masters of ceremonies.

In the Arts and Crafts section, artists paint while kids watch – then the kids try it themselves.

Professionals who demonstrate their arts are never paid to do so and they do not sell their output at the fair. The whole idea is to offer new and exciting ideas for children who are encouraged to make something by themselves (or with the help of the professionals), which the child takes home at the end of the day.

Arts and crafts for Mother Goose Land (younger children ages 2-5 years) include hammer and nail building, macaroni bead stringing, paper plate collage, banner painting, work with clay and so on.

For older kids the crafts include: pottery making with clay, macramé, wood carving, candle making, jewelry making, leather craft, sand casting, paper sculpture, stitchery and others – 42 in all. Plus an incredible Science Booth operated by the Pacific Institute of Natural Science (PINS) organization.

There is a quiet setting for disabled children to enjoy the

Animals (alive as well as wood models), puppets and puppeteers are part of Children's festival.

festival.

It is impossible to describe the magic of this very special party – a wonderful experience – for the children of the Rogue Valley.

The library has always played a key role in the success of the Children's Festival. It is the base of operations for planning and organization of the Festival and the Children's Services coordinator is the library coordinator for the event. The library acts as the sponsoring agency for the Storytelling Guild and is the organizing body as well as the advisory body for the function.

The first year of the Festival was planned for a small gathering of about fifty children to be held under a tree at Britt Garden. It was billed as "The Best of Storyhour." But six hundred showed up! Attendance quickly soared to as high as 15,000 — 3,000 at a time. Twenty-five years later, with many of the bugs worked out, attendance has evened to a manageable level of about 2,500 per session (10,000) in the park over three days. The park is only eleven acres. With this many participants, volunteers are hard put to give equal time to each child. The Festival does not promote attendance from outside the county and it is not a place for visitors to Jacksonville to "dump" kids for a glorified baby sitting period but rather as a "family experience."

136

Kids (top) love face-painting.
Incapacitated children
(lower) have equal access to
Children's Festival. They
enjoy the fun to the extent
possible.

A small gate fee ($1.50 in 1993) covers operating costs. The adult participants' only reward is the satisfaction of sharing something of themselves with children.

Gathering of the volunteers is a major project but comes easily when people want to provide new ideas for children. The process begins immediately after a July Festival. One area of con-

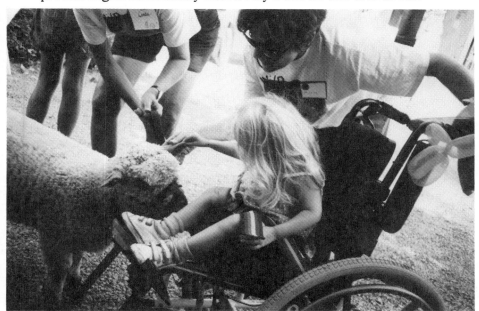

Bob Wilson, Librarian of Ashland Branch of Jackson County Library System, strolls and "fiddles" favorite tunes at Children's Festival. He plays regularly with the Rogue Valley Symphony.

cern is to identify challenges discovered then correct them. Another is to retire played-out volunteers with new people who will fill important shoes. Supplies and equipment must be arranged – either purchased, borrowed or begged. The Children's Festival consumes 2,700 volunteers (equaling 45,000 volunteer hours) to accomplish the goal. Local businesses donate materials and services. Many service organizations adopt the Festival as "community service projects." While the major list of volunteers is made up of women, many "handy-helpful-husbands" are included. Boy Scouts are on hand because troops, as well as individual Scouts, work on Community Service projects. The County Parks and Recreation Department keep the major trappings in the County warehouse during the year. A local moving crew hauls the equipment to and from the Britt grounds at Festival time.

The local chapter of the American Association of University Women (A. A. U. W.) has been involved with the event from the start. Back when the group planned for only fifty kids, this group advanced fifty dollars to begin the whole thing.

One of the absolutes of the Festival is the prohibition of fast-food stands. Says a volunteer, "The children are here to see and do, not to stuff themselves on junk foods." The A. A. U. W. has a facility operating independently of the Festival but for the convenience of the Festival, which serves cold drinks (it's usually pretty hot in July) to the kids (and hot sandwiches for hungry daddies and workers). Profits from this one-and-only food concession provide funds to refinish the stand for the next year and to fund scholarships. The partnership of Children's Festival Board and A. A. U. W. works beautifully. Some A. A. U. W. members also assist in other areas of the Festival as volunteers.

The Children's Festival and Peter Britt Music Festival have been compatible on the same grounds for years, but not at the same time, since the mid-1960's. The concerts started in 1963 and the Children's Festival in 1967.

It has taken years to get everything coordinated but those challenges, when reviewed today, just bring knowing grins. Examples: Poison oak control. Only a single electrical outlet. Just one water faucet and a need to rent portable "restrooms." But all this was not really a challenge for just a handful of kids. In recent years all these concerns have been overcome with improvements at the park.

Peter Britt loved his children and he would no doubt smile then shake his head in disbelief if he saw 10,000 of them in his front yard (in 1993) in just three days in July.

The Children's Festival is nothing short of awesome. It's a part of Jacksonville.□

19.
Music Under the Stars

The Britt Music festival commemorates Peter Britt and was founded in 1963 by Portlanders John Trudeau, a classical musician and conductor, and Sam McKinney, as advertising man and promoter.

The Festival presents a varied program each summer on a wooded hillside a few blocks from the center of town, which lovers of music enjoy while relaxing on blankets spread on the grass or in newly installed reserved seating. A few bring lawn chairs. Picnics in the park before and during the music are fine, but no clanking of glassware after the overture starts. (Seeing-Eye dogs only, please.)

The festival was the first in the Pacific Northwest and has gone on to become the premier multi-arts festival in the region.

Back in 1962 Trudeau and McKinney talked with the Jacksonville City Council, when "Curley" Graham was mayor, in an effort to convince the council that Jacksonville's spirits would indeed be lifted by such an annual event.

Don Wendt, who was on the council at that time recalls:

...you can imagine the reaction of some of us uncultured council members who were much more familiar with the tunes of the J'ville Tavern's music box than the refined compositions of Bach, Beethoven and others, which Mr. Trudeau wanted to play.

But the council listened as the visitors expounded about the atmosphere, the people and the setting of Jacksonville – especially the hillside known as "the Peter Britt property." It sounded good.

Wendt continued, "I remember making the motion to accept the offer and the council approved. But little did I realize the tremendous work" ahead of a lot of people to get it all together.

Hundreds gather to hear and see great music and musicians in Britt County Park. Picnics, while concerts are in process, are common but don't clink the wine glasses during the music!

The city didn't own the property. The council set about to show the citizens the need to get behind the effort to have a summer concert. People from all over the valley responded favorably. Wendt wrote in his Jacksonville *Nugget:*

Mrs. Bert Pree was the first president of the Britt Board along with Mr. Graham, Ben Trowbridge, Lee Konschott, Darrell Huson, Lew Tycer, George Brewer, Virginia Lusk, William Mansfield and myself. We met to decide just where to begin. First the land had to be acquired. Second a pavilion had to be built. Two major undertakings especially when no one really knew where to start. But there was a cohesion with this group, and things began to percolate when the wheels started [to roll]. First, materials were donated by merchants all over the valley. Volunteer labor was donated at a fast pace. Before we knew it, the work had begun. I'm sure many don't realize that the first Britt pavilion was built with labor from the Jackson County Prisoners. These men were 'loaned' to us to come each day and work, thanks to the efforts of county Commissioners Ed Taylor and Don Faber. I can remember taking them back to the county jail in the evening.

Progress was really noticeable. I can remember getting a D-4 cat from West Main Rental to help level the ground and make pathways around the pavilion. Even some of the prisoners were talented enough to run the heavy equipment for us. I also remember staying up till the wee hours of the morning with a crew from Pacific Light & Power Company with their auger drilling holes where benches would finally rest in front of the stage. There were many volunteers who with rakes in hand, would line up on top of the hill, and proceed to rake downward all the weeds and leaves around, leaving the grounds clean to allow people to place their blankets and chairs. I remember my father, George Wendt, donating his time for days wiring the new structure so each light would be in its proper place. Even getting water to wet down the dust was a monumental task. But function it did, and when the musicians arrived a few days early, they all had places to stay, mostly in Jacksonville where many local residents opened up their homes to these talented performers. The first night's performance was history. It was superb, not that I or some others really understood the kind of music, but because something great in Jacksonville was happening. The beer and wine flowed after the first performances, as we all knew then that the Peter Britt Music Festival should ever continue.

Thirty years later, the Britt Festival is believed to be the oldest classical festival in the United States. But there were changes in the wind. The community was split on their likes or dislikes about the Festival. There are many well-wishers, but these are now mostly out-of-town people.

Some feel the handling of "The Britt," as it's called, had become high-handed with little concern for the people of Jacksonville. While years of struggle to make the Festival successful have achieved in many areas, others, like public relations with the folks in Jacksonville, had not earned high marks. Most local people cannot see Jacksonville becoming another "cultural" and somewhat "snobbish" center, referring to Ashland's Shakespeare influence.

Initially, nearly all the music was symphonic. In recent years, responding to popular appeal and to gain more hard cash in gate receipts, while retaining symphonic works, other types of music have been added. These include several separate Festivals. At this writing in addition to the symphony, there is jazz, country, bluegrass and ballet.

On occasion there are symphonic choirs joining the orchestra. In addition, there are piano recitals; vocal soloists; quartets – instrumental and vocal – a Civil War Brass Band using Civil

War-era instruments; solo instrumentalists and singers and specialty groups. Some of the small ensembles and soloists are heard in the ballroom of the U. S. Hotel or in the historic sanctuary of the First Presbyterian Church.

Some purists squirmed when they heard that "bluegrass" and "country" music had come to Britt. And jazz! But the public needs to be served based on what the public wants. All the varieties thus far tried have brought sellout or near-sellout crowds.

> **A wheel-chair ramp is in place as is a special wheel-chair unloading and loading driveway, as well as wheel-chair access rest rooms near the stage.**

Although these varieties in types of music are heralded as separate festivals, each abuts another on the summer schedule. The Britt Music Festival has become as enticing a lure to Southern Oregon as the Shakespeare Festival in Ashland, with many visitors planning their trips to take in both.

Music lovers are now realizing that "The Britt" offers a most unique site as well as great diversity in music for a festival in the west.

The Britt Festival Association is a non-profit performing arts organization which utilizes the Britt Park under a long-term lease with Jackson County. ☐

DARDANELLES

First Post Office in Jackson County established October 19, 1852 in the cabin of Col. William G. T'Vault (1806-1869). Col. T'Vault was the Editor of Oregon's first newspaper, "The Oregon Spectator." He was Postmaster General of the Oregon Provisional Government. He died in Jacksonville during the smallpox epidemic of 1869.

—Siskiyou Pioneer Sites Foundation

20.
Post offices

The earliest post office in the vicinity of Jacksonville was Dardanelles, at a narrow place in the Rogue River, about seven miles slightly northwest of Jacksonville. William G. T'Vault was the postmaster and opened for business, in his cabin, on October 19, 1852. The settlement at Dardanelles included a stage depot and overnight hostelry, a blacksmith and a small store.

As the gold rush at Jacksonville was in full swing with lots of people to serve, a post office was opened there on February 18, 1854. With almost no one left at Dardanelles, that little post office closed on August 2nd, 1854. Because the population near there fluctuated, Dardanelles was reopened and closed a number of times during the next 24 years but closed for good on December 8, 1878. According to postal historians, there are no known examples of its postmark.

Jacksonville's postal business was conducted without fanfare in storefront offices for years but in 1968, the new brick post office was constructed on N. Oregon St. It is now overcrowded due to population increase. This is a full-service post office and has with its own unique postmark with a slogan:

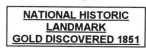

NATIONAL HISTORIC
LANDMARK
GOLD DISCOVERED 1851

On January 16, 1991, there was a 1-Day special cancellation applied to philatelic covers and general outgoing letters commemorating the centennial of the Rogue River Valley Railway. An example appears on page 90.

Since the beginning in 1854, all of the postal patrons in Jacksonville go to the post office to fetch their mail as there are no street delivery carriers. A contributing reason for this is the lack of sidewalks in the residential areas which would put letter-carriers at risk.

Early Post Offices in the immediate area and their dates of operation are:

Ashland Mills   May 17, 1855.   Dis: Jan.14, 1871
Ashland   Jan. 14, 1871   continuing 97520
Central Point   April 25, 1872   continuing 97502
Dardenelles   Oct. 19, 1852   interrupted service. Dis: Dec. 2, 1878
Jacksonville   Feb. 18, 1854   continuing 97530
Medford   Feb. 4, 1884   continuing 97501, 97504
Phoenix   Jan. 3, 1857   continuing 97535
Table Rock   Apr. 25,   1872. Dis: Aug. 7, 1874
Talent   Feb. 5, 1883   continuing 97540
Tolo   Mar. 30, 1886   interrupted service. Dis: Dec.14, 1918
Willow Springs   Aug. 12, 1864   interrupted service Dis: Feb. 25, 1888

Some examples of postmarks of Jacksonville

Postmark of Dec. 2 (no year) on 3¢ stamped envelope Scott* No. U58, a Civil War issue of 1864.

Postmark of Jan. 7, 1886 on 1¢ stamped envelope Scott* No. U116 issued in 1874.

Postmark with rosette used Oct. 17, 1888 on 2¢ Scott* No. 210 issue of 1883.

Postmark with "OREG." Apr. 27, 1904 on 2¢ Scott* No. 319 issue of 1903.

Current postmark with ZIP 97530

* Refers to *Scott Specialized Catalog of United States Stamps*

147

Appendix A.
Rogue River Indian War (1853)
—An Opinion

The discovery of gold in the Rogue River valley attracted, with some well-disposed persons, many of the most unprincipled and ungovernable white men from all countries; with few exceptions, but for these wretches, *it is believed the Indians of Oregon would have been the most Peaceable,* friendly, and *easiest managed, with proper care, of* any *uncivilized tribes within the bounds of the United States.* It is very true the Rogue River tribe was one of the few exceptions referred to; but they had felt the force of a blow administered by a command under Brevet Major P. Kearny, Captain of 1st Dragoons in 1851, near the mouth of a branch of Rogue River about 15 miles north of Table Rock, and whether this was sufficiently salutary or not, their roguish and stealing propensities afforded no just provocation, more especially when not in the commission of crime, for the infernal acts of cruelty committed upon them by some of that class of unprincipled whites, such as are always known to lurk on the confines of civilization, between the peaceable settle-ments and the Indian lodge, acknowledging no law but that of force, and in their hearts and acts far deeper down in the scale of human degradation, and far more capable of producing mischief in the settlements, because to an evil heart, there is coupled superior intelligence, than any Rogue River Indian was known to be, before or since the discovery of gold in his valley.

Does any one ask what these infernal acts of cruelty have been? And by whom have they been perpetrated? Official public documents tell us: In the autumn of 1852, "a party of citizens, under conduct of one Captain Ben. Wright, massacred over thirty Indians out of forty-eight, who had come into his camp by invitation to make a "peace."

It seems "Wright determined not to return to Yreka without bearing some evidence of success in his expedition, and having failed to find them by hunting for the Indians, he invited them to his camp by means of a squaw. Upon this invitation forty-eight came, and while there Wright directed his men to charge their rifles afresh, to make a sure fire, which was done in presence of the Indians, without exciting their suspicion, and then, upon a signal from Wright, they suddenly fired upon the Indians, and succeeded in killing about 38. The signal was the discharge of a revolver by Wright, by which he killed the two principal Indians, with whom he had been engaged in talk. Wright's men returned to town, bearing on their rifles the scalps of their victims, he reporting that he had demanded of the Indians stolen property, and on their refusal to deliver it up he had thus punished them."—(Ex. Doc. 76, 34th Cong., 3d session.)

As a natural result of this treachery, the tribe combined with the Rogue River Indians, in the following summer, and attacked a settlement near Jacksonville. We thus have what are believed to be the provocation and beginning of the Rogue River war of 1853, terminating in a fight between the Oregon volunteers, with one Captain and ten soldiers of the United States Army, under General Joseph Lane, and the Indians, on the 24th September, 1853, on the side of the mountain to the south of Battle Creek.

—Thomas Jefferson Cram, *Topographical Memoirs*

Appendix B.
A Hanging

Among the many trials held in this courtroom [in Jacksonville], none attracted more attention in their day than that of Louis O'Neil, of Ashland. On November 20, 1884, a grocer of that city, Lewis McDaniel, was killed. He was walking home shortly after dusk. His assailant lay in wait behind a fence and shot him in the head at short range with a shotgun. The subsequent arrest and trial of the alleged murderer was covered to the last detail by both the Jacksonville *Democratic Times* and the Ashland *Tidings*. It appeared to be the last instance of a hanging carried out by a country sheriff, in this case, Sheriff Abraham S. Jacobs.

On November 28, 1884, Louis O'Neill was arrested for the crime. His known enmity to the victim, and his intimacy with the victim's wife made him the logical suspect, but there were no witnesses and the long-drawn out legal proceedings never turned up any but circumstantial evidence. He never confessed to the crime. However, there seemed little doubt that he was guilty. Newspaper accounts state that he did not appear to be surprised when arrested, and did not even inquire as to the charge until later. He was implicated by boot tracks and the murder gun found nearby, which was proven to have been his. The newspapers stated that Mrs. McDaniel showed little grief [over the death of her husband].

O'Neil was tried in Jacksonville Circuit Court before Judge Lionel G. Webster, February 27, 1885. He was defended by two of the ablest lawyers in the valley. It took the jury only one hour to render a verdict of guilty. Many ladies attended the trial. On March 22, Judge Webster pronounced sentence, death by hanging in the jail yard while the prisoner still protested his innocence. Motion for a new trial was over-ruled, but O'Neil's lawyers took their case to the Supreme Court. The newspapers commented that the trial was costing a great deal of money, but it would be money "well spent if it dissipates the idea that justice is unable to overtake murderers in Southern Oregon, a natural result of the remarkable disparity between the numbers of murders and the number of convictions."

The Supreme Court upheld Judge Webster's original ruling, and O'Neil was sentenced a second time January 29, 1886. It was now reported that he was getting weak from nervousness and lack of appetite, and "might yet save the sheriff from an unpleasant duty." Meanwhile, the unhappy man was yet hoping they "would find the right man." While trying to prove his innocence he implicated Mrs. McDaniel. She was also arrested and tried for complicity, but was found not guilty. At his second appearance, O'Neil was described as looking in better health than people had been led to expect in view of his threats to starve himself to death. Execution date was set for March 12, and the sheriff requested the Jacksonville Fire Company of 27 men to act as guard. Gallows were erected west of the jail and north of the courthouse, surrounded by a tight board fence 16 feet high. Fifty or sixty people, it was promised, would be admitted. The sheriff announced his intention of performing the task personally. It was agreed that "O'Neil would do some talking now.

A relative of the condemned man, a Mr. Moon, made a desperate last minute trip to Salem to see the governor, but this hope also failed, and on the evening of the last day, O'Neil apparently gave up hope. Two Sisters of Mercy from the convent in Jacksonville had been visiting him regularly, and he now asked them to have Father Blanchet call. This the priest did at once, and according to the papers, "it is understood that he made a full confession of his sins."

Tickets were issued to qualified spectators, and the fire company, armed with rifles, presented itself. The spectacle was witnessed by about 200, including several women and two or three small children. Before the noose was attached, O'Neil was asked if he had anything to say, the priest spoke out firmly, "Mr. O'Neil has nothing to say." This was construed by the crowd as a virtual confession of guilt.

—Courtesy of Jacksonville Volunteer Fire Dept. (Archives)

150

About the Authors

Bert Webber is a research photojournalist whose specialty is what he calls "the fantastic Pacific Northwest." He graduated in journalism from Whitworth College. He earned his Master of Library Science degree from the University of Portland. He was a school librarian and teacher of Northwest History. Bert has written several dozen books a number of which have gone into multiple printings. He was also a contributor to newspapers and magazines and is listed in *Who's Who in the West* and in *Contemporary Authors*.

Margie Webber is a retired Registered Professional Nurse who earned her baccalaureate degree in Nursing from the University of Washington. She is a direct descendent of pioneers in the 1852 wagon train. She is also a fourth generation photolab assistant, as well as a copy editor. Margie is co-author, with her husband, of the present volume and of a number of other books.

The Webbers, who enjoy working with people, love to travel and do so regularly mostly as part of their research. They make their home in Oregon's Rogue River Valley – more specifically in the Bear Creek Valley – about six miles from Jacksonville. They have four children and at the moment, eight grandchildren.

For the accompanying photograph, they posed at the caved in street in Jacksonville (page 118) where one of the old-timers, who had mined for gold under his back yard in the 1930's, "tested" the earth looking to see if any was left. No gold was found. □

Bibliography

Banks, Howard C. and Len Ramp. *Gold and Silver in Oregon.* State Dept. of Geology and Mineral Ind. [Bull. 61] 1968.

Beeson, John. *The Plea For the Indians by John Beeson, Oregon's First Civil Rigjhts Advocate.* Webb Research Group. 1994

Cram, Thomas Jefferson. "Rogue River Indian War 1853" in *Ex. Doc. 76, 34th Cong., 3d session.*

Emery, Edwin. *The Press in America.* Prentice-Hall. 1962

Farnham, Wallace D. *Religion as an Influence in Life and Thought; Jackson County, Oregon 1860-1890.* Unpub. thesis. Univ. of Oregon. 1955.

Haines, Francis D. Jr. *Jacksonville, Biography of a Gold Camp.* Private print. 1981.

Halvorsen, Henry H. and Marguerite Black. *The Lodge; Jacksonville Masonic Fraternities (Oregon) Warren Lodge No. 10 A.F. & A.M.; Royal Chapter No. 4 Royal Arch Masons; Adarel Chapter No. 3 Order of Eastern Star; Warren Assembly No. 84 Order of Rainbow for Girls.* Reflected Images Publishers. 1991.

Naumes, Patrick. *St. Mary's School: A Brief History.* Private print n.d.

Richter, Adam. *A Century of Banking in the Rogue River Valley.* (Pacific Coast Banking School.) Private print 1967.

Turnbull, George S. *History of Oregon Newspapers.* Binford & Mort. 1939.

Walling, A. G. *History of Southern Oregon.* Walling. 1884.

Webber, Bert and Margie Webber. *Historic Jacksonville Alive and Well; See and Enjoy Walking Tour.* Webb Research Group. 1990.

_____.*Oregon City (By Way of the Barlow Road) At the End of the National Historic Oregon Trail.* Webb Research Group. 1993.

_____. *Single-Track to Jacksonville; The Rogue River Valley Railroad and the Southern Oregon Traction Company.* Webb Research Group. 1990.

_____. *Oregon's Great Train Holdup, Bandits Murder 4–Didn't Get A Dime!* Webb Research Group. 1988.

152

Illustration Credits

Photographs made by the authors are not credited

Index

Page numbers in **bold italic** are photographs and maps
Names of newspapers appear in *italic*

154